Research Strategies for Moving Beyond Reporting

By Sharron L. McElmeel

Linworth Publishing, Inc.
Worthington, Ohio

For Jack

Library of Congress Cataloging-in-Publication Data

McElmeel, Sharron L.
    Research strategies for moving beyond reporting / Sharron L McElmeel.
      p.   cm. — (Professional growth series)
    Includes index.
    ISBN 0-938865-54-4
    1. Library orientation for school children—United States.
  2. Library orientation for middle school students—United States.
  3. Report writing.   I. Title. II. Series.
  Z711.M4 1997
  027.8—dc20

96-34558
CIP

Published by Linworth Publishing, Inc.
480 East Wilson Bridge Road, Suite L
Worthington, Ohio 43085
Copyright © 1997 by Linworth Publishing, Inc.
Series Information:
    From The Professional Growth Series
ISBN 0-938865-54-4

Table of Contents

About the Author
Sharron L. McElmeel

Sharron L. McElmeel is a library media specialist in the Cedar Rapids (Iowa) Community School District where she works with elementary school students. She earned her B.A. in education from the University of Northern Iowa and her M.A. in library science from the University of Iowa. Honors received include being named Iowa's Reading Teacher of the Year in 1987 and nominated as a candidate for Iowa's Teacher of the Year in 1986.

Her book reviews have been aired on a national public radio affiliate. She has served on the advisory board of the International Reading Association's *Reading Journal* and is a contributing editor of the *Iowa Reading Journal*. A frequent speaker at state and national conferences, she is also a contributor to *Library Talk, The Book Report*, and other professional periodicals. Her column, "Cool Stuff on the Net" is a regular feature in *Technology Connection*. She has authored more than fifteen resource titles for library media specialists and teachers including *ABCs of an Author Illustrator Visit,* released by Linworth Publishing in 1994. McElmeel has a presence on the Internet as the moderator of Scholastic Network's library media specialist's discussion area, an educational site on the World Wide Web.

The author lives with her husband in a rural area north of Cedar Rapids, Iowa.

Chapter 1

Reports—Why Not?

In *George Washington's Breakfast* (Coward-McCann, 1969) Jean Fritz tells of a boy who wants to find out what his namesake, George Washington, ate for breakfast. The story recounts the boy's research and discovery of a document that gave the answer. The boy eventually enjoys hoecakes for breakfast just as George Washington had years before.

History is made up of the history of individuals. History gains immediacy through handwritten letters, official documents, applications, and other records created at the time of the event. For example, early inventions are documented through patent applications, drawings, and letters discussing the invention. Scientific discoveries are documented in the scientists' handwritten memos, articles, and letters to colleagues. Primary documents provide us with a direct link to the events of the past.

Others may want to learn about a grandfather or grandmother; and their search takes on meaning when they uncover a handwritten letter from the grandparent—describing hardships of their early life in the midwest.

Our own history is reflected in accounts of our lives. An account of a person's own early days is made meaningful by examining birth certificates, baby book entries, letters to relatives, and interviews with people who knew the person as a youngster.

Primary research is conducted and interpreted firsthand. To find out how bees build their honeycombs one could read someone else's observations or observe the process for herself and then report on the primary research of direct observation. Do dogs really wag the tip of their tail when they are ready to attack another animal? One could read others' reports or observe for herself. What kind of support does the mayoral candidate have in your city? Why depend on secondhand information? Conduct your own survey on the candidate's support. Does the community support establishing a little league soccer club? Don't depend on the local newspaper's letters to the editor. Conduct your own poll. If the information is important, primary research can provide definite answers.

Welcome to *Research Strategies for Moving Beyond Reporting*—lessons for teaching primary research. These lessons are designed to introduce elementary and middle grade students to basic research processes and to provide opportunities for them to practice those processes. Students will learn to formulate questions, make predictions based on accumulated knowledge, utilize data gathering techniques, organize, and record data. They will analyze results, conclusions, interpret information, and identify implications for further research. A variety of projects are suggested for sharing their learning, including written presentations, videos, museum-type displays, computer-generated slide shows, Web pages on the Internet, and other media appropriate to the project's identified task.

Research or Reporting

"Research" in elementary and middle schools often comprises reading books, searching the Internet, or otherwise accessing information already gathered by others and then *rewording* that information into a *report* on the topic. The process is one of regurgitating the findings and ideas of those who conducted the original study and published their own conclusions. The ideas and lesson plans that follow will help students move beyond the rewording process, the traditional report, to identify an original task, conduct their own primary research and consult primary sources for themselves. The resulting product will have special meaning for the student who compiled it. Many erroneously consider "research skills" to be synonymous with "library skills." However, skills in using the library or library media center fall short of providing skills for the entire research process. Much research depends on a knowledge of library skills but research also has many other components.

Library Skills—A Continuum

Library skills have traditionally focused on accessing information within the library media center's walls. Resources within the library are immense and a major component of research requires skills necessary to assess books and nonprint items. In this age of technology it is important that access to an encyclopedia includes an awareness of the purpose of it and knowledge about accessing it in print as well as the electronic form (CD-ROM). But whether the encyclopedia is on a computer screen or in a book, the content will be similar. Electronic reference sources (either CD-ROM or online searchable indexes) usually allow for Boolean searches, which has some advantage for some information sources. In many libraries information is also available through access to outside libraries or sources via telephone lines or direct connections. Access to public libraries, their catalog and magazine indexes is one of the most valuable resources available in some school libraries. Budget cuts have kept many elementary and middle school libraries from subscribing to the more expensive indexes to general periodicals. Periodical subscriptions have been severely reduced. Through a modem access to the public library's periodical indexes, students can often obtain citations to periodicals that contain information for their research. In some instances they can obtain full texts or summations of the articles. Internet access, if available, can yield tremendous amounts of information, although it must be assessed in terms of appropriateness, credibility, authorship, verified accuracy, and usefulness to the task. Sometimes the Internet can yield information in a reasonable time; at other times the search can take hours. The bookmark function available as part of most graphic Internet browsers can help students locate viable information quickly, but someone must identify appropriate locations for bookmarks. Access and time for searching will play an important role in utilizing this source.

Library skills such as accessing the traditional and technology-related sources are only part of learning to do research. To accomplish research the student needs to identify the task or question, and read, interview, listen, take notes, cite sources, access and restructure information, brainstorm ideas with peers, find nontraditional sources of information, use the telephone, and ask appropriate questions.

The following continuum represents some standard library skills published by school districts, publishers, and individual authors. There is nothing sacred about the continuum or about the placement of skills. In some schools kindergarten students have learned where the fiction books were located while other primary readers located books by particular topics of interest and quickly learned general Dewey Decimal sections. Some third graders learned to access the public library's catalog, from a remote access point, while some fourth and fifth graders still struggled with the LMC's computer catalog. Some students learned to utilize search engines of the Internet while others were dealing with bookmarks and linking sites. The library skills that students learn is based on assessment of need and availability of resources.

In addition to group-learned library skills, individual students need many additional general skills for research. The library media specialist and the classroom teacher both play a role in helping students work through a research project, recognizing that library skills per se are only one component of the total research picture. Those teaching research strategies must be aware of the students' pre-existing library skills to use those skills in the research project. The following continuum provides a baseline for that information, recognizing the variations of individual schools and centers. Students will also have had individualized needs during their school years and their information may or may not coincide with the planned scope of skills. Collaboration between the library media specialist and the classroom teacher will refine the skills list for specific research tasks.

Library Media Center Skills

Kindergarten-Grade 1

I. Location Skills
   A. Organization of Materials
      1. Knows that materials in the library media center have a specific location.
      2. Is developing an understanding of her or his own responsibility for keeping materials in order.
      3. Knows that books designated "E" or *Easy* are arranged in alphabetical order by the author's last name.
      4. Can locate a book in the "E" section by the author's last name.
   B. Fiction and Nonfiction
      1. Knows that "E" books are fiction.
      2. Knows the location of the "E" fiction section.
      3. Knows the location of the nonfiction section.

    4. Knows the location of specific nonfiction areas (example: pets, dinosaurs, folklore).

    5. Has an initial understanding of the difference between fiction and nonfiction.

  C. Checking Out Library Materials

    1. Is aware of the procedure for checking out materials (books, videotapes, cassettes).

    2. Knows the procedure for returning materials.

  D. Nonprint Materials

    1. Knows that the library media center has video- and audiocassette tapes.

    2. Can use an audiocassette recorder to listen to an audiotape.

    3. Can use a videocassette recorder to view a videotape.

  E. Community

    1. Knows of the availability of other libraries in the community.

    2. Is aware that she or he may borrow materials at other libraries.

II. Interpretation Skills

  A. Evaluation and Selection Techniques

    1. Knows that the library has books to borrow and use.

    2. Knows that children of all ages and adults use the library.

    3. Is able to choose books of interest.

    4. Can select books that she or he is able to read or retell.

    5. Takes proper care of books.

    6. Follows circulation procedures.

  B. Listening and Viewing Skills

    1. Is developing the ability to attend to storytelling.

    2. Is developing the ability to respond to sights and sounds.

  C. Literature Appreciation

    1. Knows that there are a variety of books in the library media center: books that tell a story or give information about a specific topic.

    2. Can name at least five favorite books by title.

    3. Can name at least five favorite main book characters.

    4. Is able to name at least five favorite authors or illustrators by name.

    5. Is developing the ability to discuss similarities and differences in story grammar.

    6. Is developing the ability to recognize illustrative style.

    7. Is developing the ability to recognize story genre, especially fiction, nonfiction, and folktales.

    8. Is developing regular daily reading habits.

Grades 2-3

I. Location Skills

  A. Organization of Materials

    1. Is able to locate and replace books in the "E" section by the author's last name.

    2. Can locate general fiction books by the author's last name.

    3. Knows that the spine label tells where the book is located on the shelf.

4. With assistance, is able to locate books on specific topics in the nonfiction section of the library.
5. Understands that items in the library collection are listed in the catalog by subject, author, and title.
6. Is able to locate a book in the library media center given the call numbers listed in the catalog.
7. Is able to locate a specific book by using the library's catalog of holdings.
8. Knows that the card or computer entry for a specific book contains information about the book, for example: publisher, date, annotation subject matter or story synopsis.

B. Fiction and Nonfiction
1. Is able to distinguish fiction from nonfiction.
2. Is able to locate fiction books by specific authors.
3. Is able to locate nonfiction books by specific topics.
4. Is familiar with the call numbers and their relation to the book's location on the shelf.
5. Understands the general shelf arrangement of library materials.
6. Can identify selected Dewey Decimal sections in the nonfiction area, for example: folklore, space, dinosaurs, animals.

C. Reference Collection
1. Can identify two types of reference tools: encyclopedia and dictionary.
2. Is able to locate the reference section in the library.
3. Can use the alphabetical order in the dictionary.
4. Is able to use the index of encyclopedias to locate information within the encyclopedias' volumes.

D. Biographical Sources
1. Is able to locate information about a person with some assistance.
2. Is aware that individual biographies are shelved in the biography section, in alphabetical order by the subject's last name.

E. Periodicals
1. Is familiar with the terms *magazine* and *periodical*.
2. Is aware of the availability of periodicals including newspapers.

F. Community
1. Knows of reading and story activities available at other area libraries.
2. Is aware that she or he may borrow materials at other libraries.

II. Interpretation Skills
A. Evaluation and Selection Techniques
1. Is able to select books of individual interest.
2. Can select books that she or he is able to read.
3. Is able to select books of appropriate content for specific purposes.
4. Is familiar with various forms of literature.
5. Knows some favorite authors and their works.
6. Shows discrimination in selecting books.

B. Parts of a Book
1. Can identify a book cover.
2. Can identify a book's spine and spine label.
3. Can identify a book's title page.
4. Can identify a book's author, illustrator, and title.
5. Can identify the dedication and other book features such as glossary and index.
6. Is able to locate the book's publisher and copyright date.
C. Research and Reporting
1. Is able to look up information in a general encyclopedia, either print or CD-ROM version.
2. Is able to locate nonfiction books on a specific topic, with assistance.
3. Can predict library-related or community resources that might contain the needed information.
D. Literature Appreciation
1. Knows that a variety of books are available in the library.
2. Can relate the point of a story to her or his own experience.
3. Is able to identify at least five favorite books by title or main character and list the author and illustrator for each.
4. Can draw comparisons between two or more stories.
5. Is able to recognize an illustrator's style.
6. Is able to recognize story genre, for example: folklore, realistic fiction, humor, mysteries.
7. Demonstrates reading habit by reading unassigned material each day.
8. Is knowledgeable about authors writing in student's interest area or reading level.

Grades 4-5
I. Location Skills
A. Utilizing the Library Catalog
1. Is able to use the library's general subject, author, title, catalog function to locate a specific book.
2. If system is automated is able to use Boolean functions to search for materials that include references to a specific topic.
3. Is able to independently locate materials in the library by using the call numbers.
4. Is able to substitute, broaden, or narrow own subject terminology language used in the library's catalog to facilitate location of material.
5. Can recognize the appropriateness of subject headings proposed for locating materials.
B. Fiction and Nonfiction
1. Recognizes and can define the two main categories of materials: fiction and nonfiction.
2. Knows that "B" designates individual biographies (nonfiction).
3. Knows that "E" designates a book in the *Easy* section (picture

books, often fiction), *FIC* designates fiction titles, *REF* designates reference materials, and books with numbers in the call numbers designate nonfiction titles.

C. Dewey Decimal System
  1. Understands that the purpose of the Dewey Decimal system is to bring together materials of the same literary form and subject.
  2. Can locate materials using call numbers with Dewey Decimal numbers.
  3. Is acquainted with the ten main classes of Dewey numbers.
  4. Can name and locate the Dewey section for at least one class of nonfiction books, for example, sports (700s) or folklore (300s).
D. Reference Collection
  1. Knows the nature of books in the reference collection.
  2. Is able to locate information in reference sources.
      a. Encyclopedias (print and electronic editions)
          (1) Is able to use an encyclopedia for answering background information questions.
          (2) Can use an encyclopedia to find an overview of a specific topic.
          (3) Is able to use the index and alphabetical arrangement of a printed encyclopedia to locate information.
          (4) Is able to use the Boolean search technique to locate information in an electronic encyclopedia.
      b. Dictionaries
          (1) Can obtain definitions from dictionary entries.
          (2) Can use alphabetical order and guide words.
          (3) Is familiar with the unabridged dictionary.
      c. Almanacs
          (1) Knows that almanacs contain charts, tables, statistics, and brief factual information.
          (2) Can locate and use the index to locate that information.
      d. Atlases
          (1) Knows that atlases are sources of maps.
          (2) Can derive information on a specific location using an atlas.
E. Biographical Sources
  1. Can distinguish between a biography and an autobiography.
  2. Is able to locate biographical information in general or multivolume reference books, for example: *Bookpeople: A Second Album* (Libraries Unlimited, 1990) and *Something About the Author* (Gale).
  3. Is able to identify sources of biographical information from alternative resources, for example: interviews, newspapers, periodicals, letters and other primary documents.
  4. Knows that collective biographies are located in the 920s of the nonfiction section.
  5. Is developing an awareness of periodicals as a source of information and pleasure reading.

    F. Indexes
1. Realizes that the catalog is an index to the library or LMC.
2. Knows the function of a book index.
3. Knows that indexes are generally at the end of books.
4. Can use the index to reference books and books in the general collection.

    G. Evaluation
1. Is developing the ability to determine the scope, arrangement, and purpose of a reference work.
2. Is developing the ability to assess credibility and relative importance of specific information in relation to author credibility, copyright date, and comprehensiveness.

II. Interpretation Skills
    A. Evaluation and Selection Techniques
1. Is familiar with various forms of literature.
2. Is able to select materials for a specific purpose.
3. Is acquainted with authors and their works.

    B. Research and Reporting Techniques
1. Can locate materials to discover what others have learned about a topic.
2. Refines ability to predict a resource's appropriateness for specific research questions.
3. Is able to use ideas gained through research to restructure information and answer a specific question or contribute to a specific problem.
4. Is able to access and use reference sources outside of the immediate library where they are, for example: access the local public libraries' catalogs by modem or access and use specific reference locations on the Internet.

    C. Literature Appreciation
1. Is familiar with various forms of literature.
2. Can interpret meaning from literature and can relate the experience to past experiences or information.
3. Recognizes reading as a means of gaining information, pursuing interests, and relaxation.
4. Reads each day.

Grades 6-7

Instruction during these two grades should concentrate on refining and maintaining the previously learned skills in literature and research. Teachers should continue to develop students' habit of reading and using library skills within the total context of research and investigation. Students who can use technologically based resources should begin to display independence in access and utilization. Others should be introduced to all available book and technology resources.

Specific instruction should introduce:
1. Use of periodical indexes.
2. Use of new specialized reference sources in the library's collection.
3. Use of electronic resources available through the library.

Grades 8-12

During these years all library skills taught previously are reinforced in course work and reviewed individually throughout curriculum areas. Reading will be encouraged and motivated through book talks, reading promotions, and book reviews.

<u>Notes</u>

Chapter 2
A First Step—Beginning the Research

One of the first steps in a research project is to acquaint or review with students the areas most available to them in the library media center. Other resources such as telephone access, area libraries, people and the Internet should also be discussed. The following library skills and general areas of the library media center should be reviewed with the students. Library skills should be taught within the context of an authentic question or need. Therefore the following is a reminder of skills that may be emphasized as students move through activities in the following chapters. For example, second-grade students would have a working acquaintance with the "E" section (*Easy* section, sometimes referred to as *picture book section*) of the library media center. As primary students learn about certain authors and want to read their books, the teacher or librarian has a natural teaching opportunity when the students come to the library media center in search of those books. An interest in baseball will lead a student to use the catalog subject function to locate baseball books in the nonfiction area. The following discussion about sections of the library media center will assist instructors in clarifying characteristics of each section and help students build knowledge of resources they may use in their research. A brief overview will give student researchers the knowledge to find sections and information at the point of need. The mini-research lessons (Chapter 3) will suggest other types of available resources.

General Arrangement of the Library Media Center (LMC)

- *E* (Easy) Section—In general, books in this section are picture books, most often fiction about people, places, things, and events. Some library media centers place heavily illustrated nonfiction books here as well. Nonfiction authors with heavily illustrated works include: Gail Gibbons, Jerry Palotta, Aliki, Caroline Arnold, and Seymour Simon. The first line of the call letters and numbers on the book's spine will be an *E*. The second line will be the first three letters of the author's last name.

- Fiction Section—Fiction books have the main purpose of telling a story. Although some books include facts or historically true incidents, the imaginative stories have been created by the author. Facts or real people in fiction are literary devices to give the story credibility. The call letters on the spines of these books most often have *FIC* on the first line and the first three letters of the author's last name on the second line.

- Nonfiction Section—Most small public libraries and school library media centers use the Dewey Decimal System to organize and categorize books by subject. (See Dewey Decimal Chart in Appendix A.) Although some nonfiction section books are not informational (for example: myths (292); folklore (398.2); poetry and plays (811-817); literature (800s)), most books in the nonfiction section provide information about specific topics. A nonfiction book spine will have the Dewey Decimal number on the top line and the first three letters of the author's last name on the second line.

- Biography Section—According to the Dewey Decimal System of Classification biographies should be in the 920 section of the library media center. However, many years ago it was determined that those browsing the biography section were more interested in the book's subject than its author. In the 920 section, the books would be shelved by the author's last name. Consequently, these books were removed from the history shelves and given the special designation, *B*, standing for biography (as well as autobiography). In this special section, the first line of the call number is *B*, and the second line comprises the first three letters of the *subject's* last name.

- Reference Section—Books in the reference section are arranged and organized to provide quick answers to specific quests for data. The best reference books are organized alphabetically or are thoroughly indexed. Both organizational structures allow the researcher to go directly to topic entry. Biographical references often are arranged alphabetically. Books such as almanacs are thoroughly indexed. The index will direct the researcher to the page with a particular piece of information. Since references are not the type of books read from cover to cover but accessed for pieces of information or (as in the case of encyclopedias) brief articles about a topic, most libraries and library media centers restrict the checkout of these books. Most reference titles must be used in the library. Teachers should check with the library media specialist, however, because some library media centers allow patrons to check out a reference book for a class period or overnight. Others may not allow the current edition of a reference volume to be checked out but will permit borrowing earlier volumes of an encyclopedia or last year's almanac which may contain similar information.

Electronic Resources

- Connections to other libraries via modem/direct connection/ Internet—When a book is not available in the school's library media center it may be helpful to know if it is available nearby. Periodical indexes and periodical abstracts are available in various libraries. A school's modem access to the city public library may also access the Library of Congress catalog and periodical indexes, featuring brief abstracts of selected articles. If such a service is available in your area, student researchers may obtain important information by searching the periodical indexes or the Library of Congress. The Internet also offers access to the Library of Congress through its universal resource locator code (URL). Those who wish can reach the Library of Congress with the "open" command on *Netscape* or another graphic Internet access using the URL http://www.loc.gov/. From that home page, searchers must go to "LC Online systems" and click on the phrase "Z39.50fill-in form"—from that point instructions are obvious. Students can type the book title or author's name in the blank, select, and the computer will search the LC catalog and return the requested information. Searchers can go directly to the search form by using http://lcweb.loc.gov/Z3950.

- Obtaining access—Young researchers may need to be instructed in the procedure for actually obtaining the access. They need to know from whom they can obtain access, under what circumstances, and how to request access. For example, in some school systems access to the Internet is controlled by individual passwords that only approved users receive. If the approved user (always an adult educator) is willing, a student may access the Internet, however, the password holder must activate the connection and remain available to supervise. Regardless of the procedure in an individual school, students must learn the logistics. Young students may not realize that they need only to ask, and must be made aware of possibilities and procedures for access. It is not enough for them to know that the Internet connection exists. If it is to be a viable resource, they must know how they can get access to it.

- Other electronic resources—CD-ROMS are reference materials on a disc. Encyclopedias such as *Grolier's* or *Compton's* are often available in the library media center computer reference station. These electronic catalogs have the advantage of allowing students to search by keyword. The overview of the library media center should include information on the availability of these sources. Procedure and how-to sessions may need to be scheduled so that students learn to use these resources.

- Miscellaneous—Resources not strictly considered references are sometimes equally important to a young researcher. For example, if a student needs to contact a business person, professional, or a community agency, that contact needs to take place during the school day. The researcher must learn the procedure for using a telephone during the school day. What is the policy for student use of office or LMC telephones? Other miscellaneous resources may include the telephone book and the daily newspaper.

Library Media Center Catalog

Instructors will want to review search methods by author, subject, and title.
The subject tag is appropriate for some keywords only if one believes that the
center will have a book entirely about that subject. For example, books about
George Washington will be listed under *Washington, George* but other
information about this man may be available in books about Presidents. The
Boolean search process may be important in this review if the LMC is
automated and the computer catalog offers this function. To assist in reviewing
the card catalog, Appendix B contains Search Cards that can be reproduced and
kept on file in the classroom. During the review period the instructor may ask
students to select a card from the file, go to the LMC and use the catalog to
locate a book that corresponds with the author, subject, or title on the card.
Because most automated library media centers have two to five computer
catalog stations available and a finite number of card catalog drawers in a small
space, it is appropriate to schedule one to four students in the LMC at one time.
With Search Cards in their hands students will have the correct spelling of the
word or name they need to look up. Library media personnel will be readily
able to assist the students who have a specific task to accomplish. Library
media center's collections vary so some cards may not lead to the location of a
specific item. If a student returns to the classroom without material on the
subject or the title, the instructor should check with the library media specialist
to verify that that subject, name, or title would *not* have led to any library
materials. In the case of subject searches, students may not find a book on a
narrow subject but might find a book about a broader category and within that
book a chapter on the specific topic. That situation would encourage students
to use a Boolean search to locate a book, and to use the index within the
identified book to locate the subject.

Chapter 3
Mini-Research Lessons

Mini-research questions help students learn to think about a multitude of sources that might yield information. The mini-research questions suggested in this section include notes to assist the teacher in guiding researchers to appropriate resources and, in many cases, primary documents and sources to answer the questions. At this stage, we will not classify resources as primary or secondary. Lesson plans following the mini-research lessons suggest a sequential approach to introduce students to the concepts of primary and secondary research. Once the distinction is made this text will provide a plan of action designed to guide students through the steps of a research project using primary and secondary sources. The sequential lessons will help researchers in: Selecting and defining the task; Predicting strategies for gathering information; Information gathering; Recording selected information; Restructuring the information for the task; and Evaluating and showcasing the information (S.P.I.R.R.E.).

Challenging Students to Research

Many elementary students believe that every quest for information answered is in a book and the way to locate any book is to look in the library media center's catalog. At their age they don't know that the topic might be too obscure for authors to devote an entire book to the subject. For example, one youngster was sent to the library media center to learn the name of the mayor of Cedar Rapids. The mayor had been elected in November, had taken office in early January, and the date of the research was January 15. The library media center was a small elementary center that did not have back issues of local newspapers. Even if it had, few newspapers have indexing of a nature that allows anything but an inefficient page-by-page search. The student thought he could use keywords and perhaps could find some information on the computer catalog using those keywords. The student identified mayor and Cedar Rapids as appropriate keywords. The only problem with the search process was the student's choice of an inappropriate resource for the topic. Not only would the center not have had published material to report such a recent event but neither the town nor the mayor herself is a significant enough subject to warrant an entire book. A research conference with the student rescued this question from the frustration bank. After explaining to the student the problems with using the library media center catalog to locate this information, the librarian asked the student to consider where she might find the answer. She suggested perhaps the newspaper would have the mayor's name or perhaps she could call the mayor's office and ask the secretary for the name and the correct spelling. She did and she got her answer. That is primary research. Another group of students was beginning to collect information for a Web site on literacy. Their topic was *newly literate people*. They decided to interview people who were newly literate and share some thoughts of those newly literate people on the Web site. The immediate question was, "Where will we find some people, who have just learned to read and write to interview?" Their first response was to look under *literate* on the computer catalog. The media specialist asked the researchers what they expected to find if they typed in *literate?* None of them knew. They had been given the keyword instruction often enough that whenever they wanted to find information, they had used the topic rather than the question as their guide. It did not occur to the students that even if they found a book on literacy, it would not have the information they needed. They needed names and addresses or telephone numbers of local people who were newly literate and who would be willing to be interviewed. As facilitator of this project the library media specialist attempted to help the students back up and think through the process. She suggested they think about the adults who have recently learned to read and write. Perhaps the first step would be to think about how the new skills were acquired. The students realized their solution as they thought about what they were really trying to find. At this stage they were not trying to learn about literacy, they were trying to find people who had recently learned to read and write. They figured that someone probably taught the adults and that teacher might give them names of persons willing to be interviewed. The students decided to find local programs that might have taught adults to read. The group previously had discussed the fact that the public library had many community references and specialized reference books, and students were aware of the public library's role as a quick reference source. One student called the public library and asked if there were adult literacy programs in the area. The response led the researchers to a local community college where students telephoned a program director. The program director put them in touch with two individuals who were pleased to tell their story. Once the students had arranged for an interview, they constructed their questions. From the interview, they obtained much of the information they needed. Then they gathered background information from the literacy program's brochure, which they obtained from the program director. The primary research, the interview with newly literate adults, was the key to a successful and meaningful research experience.

The following pages suggest mini-research questions that will encourage students to predict a strategy, find, and verify the answer. Some questions will lead the researcher to the library media center's catalog but they could lead elsewhere as well. The goal of the research questions is to provide quick introductions to a variety of resources and strategies. Once researchers learn about a variety of resources and ways to obtain information they will be ready for more extensive research projects.

A key component of the mini-research lessons is to show students the thinking process for predicting resources that they may use to find the appropriate answer to the question. For that reason, the question in each mini-research lesson is provided in large print in Appendix C, so that teachers may make copies for students or an overhead transparency to share with a large group. The transparency should be displayed, predictions should be made for strategies to use in finding the answer, and the answer should be sought using the suggested sources. For group activities, the teacher may wish to form smaller cooperative discussion groups to predict strategies. At the end of the day or the following day, but after the students have attempted to find the answer, the students should engage in research talk, a discussion among researchers exchanging ideas, verifying results, and relaying pros and cons of using various sources. Research talk gives student researchers the opportunity to share what sources they tried and what kinds of successes they had.

Teachers may need to review etiquette for telephone calls. Appendix A includes a transparency master that reviews procedures for an interview. A phone log master is also available. It is a good idea to have each caller fill out the log to keep track of telephone calls, particularly if toll fees are involved. In addition, if the log is available to the person answering return calls, that person will have the information needed to take the message and pass it on to the appropriate researcher.

Suggested research questions offer models of questions that lead researchers to types of resources which they might need as they later pursue more extensive topics. The notes following each research question provide at least one path toward the solution. Other techniques are possible and creative methods of solving the research question should be encouraged.

Mini-Research Questions and Teacher Notes

Mini-Research #1: A third-grade class went on a field trip to a sheep farm. They watched sheep being sheared and got to feel the wool. The next day one child was found to have head lice. His mother was upset thinking that her son probably got the head lice from the sheep. Is that possible?

Notes for the Teacher—This question arose one year in a midwest city. The researchers found definitions for head lice. They even found magnified photographs of the creature but they could not locate an answer to whether or not lice from sheep could be transferred to people. They called the public library and asked reference librarians to check medical references. The answer did not seem to be anywhere. But there is an answer and it was found by consulting a veterinarian. The answer was *no*, head lice cannot be transferred from animals to humans. Guide your students through a similar thinking and action process. When the telephone call suggestion surfaces consider modeling appropriate telephone etiquette. A transparency master to use for reviewing telephone etiquette and a log for recording calls from school telephones are in Appendix A.

Mini-Research #2: In order to enroll in an electronic media class a student must prove his or her age. Since there is an age requirement for this class, the school needs written proof of the student's date of birth. If you were this student, how could you prove your birthdate?

Notes for the Teacher—Most adults know that a student's birth certificate will provide the necessary proof. However, some students may not know about the existence of birth certificates. Traditionally schools have accepted similar official documents such as a hospital birth certificate or a baptismal certificate, signed and dated by officials at that institution. Some students will have copies of their birth certificate available. However, assuming that they do not, most individuals can obtain a copy of their own birth certificate (or those for which they have a natural interest—mother, father), from the department of vital statistics in their birth state. Most states have birth registration laws that require clerks of court in each county to register the dates of birth of all persons born in that county and reported to the clerk's office. The first such law was passed in the state of Georgia in 1823. Each birth registered is usually kept at the county seat in the county where the birth took place; but the birth registry is also archived at the state level. Adopted children will be able to receive their birth certificate, listing their adoptive parents. Requests for copies of the official document can be made to the clerk of courts in the appropriate county. Or, requests can be sent to the state. Usually the requests must be accompanied by a fee ranging from $4 to $10. The Department of Vital Statistics for each state is often among the government offices in the state capital. A student born in Iowa might request his or her birth certificate from the county seat in the county where he or she was born or from the Department of Vital Statistics, State of Iowa, Des Moines, Iowa. Zip codes can be obtained by calling the post office in your area, using a zip code directory (found in larger libraries) or accessing the zip code directory on the Internet (<*http://lcweb.loc.gov*> or <*http://www.usps.gov/postofc/pstoffc.htm*>). While most students will not want to spend the dollars to obtain their birth certificates, they can locate the appropriate address to which a letter should be sent requesting it. Their first task will be to determine in what city, county, and state they were born. Asking their parents will give them the city and state. From that information a United States atlas should yield the county. If the county seat is not available in a state almanac or state official registry, the student may locate the name of the state capital and then find the zip code using a zip code directory. Once the state capital and zip code are located, students can write the appropriate letter. This is an opportunity for instructing students in the format the U.S. Postal Service requests for addressing envelopes. (See Appendix A for "Addressing an Envelope" and for "Abbreviations.")

Mini-Research #3: What is the most difficult part of being a
_____(career)_____ ? What is the best part of being a ___(career)_____ ?

Notes for the Teacher—Identify a career that you might consider having as an adult. Members of the class may identify occupations that they may wish to consider holding. Preliminary information should be located in secondary sources. Information including basic education requirements, average salary, and the career benefits should be recorded. After the background information is located, if the students are still interested in the career, they will want to learn firsthand the best and the worse parts of being in that specific career. Each student should locate a person engaged in that occupation and ask to interview her or him. Names of people to interview may come from discussion among class members or through the telephone book, referrals from union and professional organizations, and referrals from companies that employ people in that occupation. The interview could be conducted by mail or by telephone.

Different situations and careers will require decisions concerning the interview method. As appropriate, review interviewing techniques and letter writing procedures.

Mini-Research #4: Each year the American Library Association presents the Newbery Award to an author and the Caldecott Award to an illustrator. Who won this year's awards? What were the titles of the books that earned the award for the author or illustrator?

Notes for the Teacher—Encyclopedias, children's literature texts, and periodicals will list the winners from previous years. Posters developed by various publishing representatives will display the winners up to the current year. The awards are announced each year in late January or early February. Very recent up-to-date information will be needed to locate the current year's winners, especially if this task is used in the beginning months of the year. Those who have access to periodical indexes will find that articles published sometime after the end of January or the first week of February likely include the list of the new winners. The Internet can also yield information through the American Library Association's Web site (http://www.ala.org/index.html). The news release announcing these awards will provide the information needed. Other children's literature sites on the Internet will also have the information after a month or so. If your public library has a telephone reference service, a call to the service may also yield the answer. One should allow students the same resources as adults might use—including reference sources such as the public library services.

Mini-Research #5: Construct a three-generation family tree: You >— mother>—grandmother and grandfather>— father>grandmother/grandfather.

Notes for the Teacher—Interviews with parents and grandparents should yield this information. It is a common topic associated with genealogy. However, some teachers are reluctant to ask students to deal with such topics given situations involving an absent or unknown parent, fractured families, and adoption. If this is one of many choices class members are given, students who wish will deal with the topic and others will not choose it. Some parents express appreciation for the opportunity to discuss the young person's other parent in a positive manner. Choice is the key to keeping the experience comfortable for the researcher. Provide each student with a family tree form (see Appendix A). Ask the researchers to use separate sheets of paper to write about each of the people on their family tree. Birth and other significant dates including death, if appropriate, should be included. The term maiden name is inappropriate and should be replaced with birth name which can apply to both men and women. For mothers, grandmothers, fathers and grandfathers, the birth name should be placed on the form. Researchers may tell about their own childhoods, their family, or a favorite family story. After draft copies have been revised, corrections made, and final copies created, a cover, a title page, and a final copy of the family tree should be bound together into a book.

Mini-Research #6: Locate the title of a book written by Jacqueline Briggs Martin.

Notes for the Teacher—If your school's catalog does not yield the title of a book by Martin, try to access the catalog of a larger library that has children's books. Area libraries may have a title by Jacqueline Briggs Martin. Martin's books will be listed in the Library of Congress catalog. To access the Library of Congress through the Internet, use the "open" command on *Netscape* or another graphic access and type in the LOC address (http://www.loc.gov/). When that home page is displayed, go to "LC Online systems" and click on the phrase "Z39.50fill-in form" then follow the instructions given. Put the author's name in the blank, select, and the computer will search the LC catalog and return the information. To go directly to the search form use the following Library of Congress URL (http://lcweb.loc.gov/Z3950). Often the local or state public library catalogs can be accessed through a modem connection. Check with your local public library to find out if such a connection exists.

Mini-Research #7: How many gallons of milk are consumed each day in your school?

Notes for the Teacher—This information can be obtained by interviewing the cafeteria workers who are responsible for selling the milk to children at school. However, the question states, "consumed." A count of the number of cartons of milk sold will not necessarily indicate all the milk that was consumed. Children will need to discuss ways to determine how much of the milk sold was actually consumed. Solutions may include pouring unconsumed milk into a gallon bucket and tallying the quantity, converting the number of cartons sold into a quantity, and subtracting the amount of milk not consumed from the amount of milk sold.

Mini-Research #8: What is the average number of children in the families of members of your class?

Notes for the Teacher—To calculate the average number of children in the families one must interview a member of each family. The information is probably not available anywhere else. The person completing this research should interview each student to find out how many children are in his or her family. With the number for each family recorded, the numbers should be totalled and divided by the number of families represented. The numerical solution will yield the average number of children in class members' families.

Mini-Research #9: How many books were checked out of the school library media center today before noon?

Notes for the Teacher—If the library media center is automated, the system will record the number of checkouts during the day. In fact, most systems can generate detailed lists indicating how many books in various categories were checked out to a certain point in the day. If the media center is not automated, the task will be more difficult. The actual checkout cards must be tallied. Students should consult with the library media specialist about the best way to collect this information.

Mini-Research #10: In a ten-minute period of individual reading time, how many words are read by members of your class?

Notes for the Teacher—First the class must schedule a ten-minute period for individual reading. Once the period is completed, the number of words can be ascertained by: (1) Each reader counting the exact number of words that were read. This may work if the books are picture, or minimal text books. However, it will consume an inordinate amount of time if the books are novels or have many words on a page. In that case: (2) Each student can count the number of words on one to five pages and then average the number of words per page of that particular book. Each student can multiply the average number by the number of pages read to get a logical estimate of the number of words. The totals for all students should be added together to obtain the total estimate for the class. The class should come to a consensus of whether the estimate is accurate enough to satisfy the question or whether each word must be counted individually.

Mini-Research #11: In what year was your school established and how many different educators have been principal of your school? Name the principals and dates each were in charge of the school.

Notes for the Teacher—Often a school will have archives, a plaque on a wall or some other documentation within the building that lists the principals. If that is not the case, the district's central office probably will have some information. Depending on the school district, the central staff person who has the information will vary. A logical place to begin is to ask the assistant superintendent in charge of buildings and grounds when the building first was opened. The personnel office will probably have staff information or staff directories. It may take several phone calls to learn who has the information and request it. The information can be displayed on a chart showing the names and dates of each principal since the school opened.

Mini-Research #12: What was the headline in the local newspaper on the day you were born?

Notes for the Teacher—Depending on the student's age, the strategy for locating this information will vary. Some youngsters may have a baby book with the information preserved. Others might have to visit a local newspaper's archives (if they exist) while others may locate the headline in the microfilm department of the local library. Many libraries now archive major and local newspapers on microfilm and provide machines for reading and printing the film.

Mini-Research #13: When and how did your family (paternal or maternal) arrive in the United States? Or what is the earliest record of a member of your family in the United States? Tell about the situation surrounding the arrival or about your ancestors' early days in America.

Notes for the Teacher—Recent immigrants will have a much different story to tell than Native Americans whose history goes farther into the past than any record will, in probability, document. This question may encourage interviews of older family members, who might remember stories passed down from earlier members. The interviews will be primary research and should result in some form of text about the researcher's family.

Mini-Research #14: When did you first walk, say your first word, and get your first tooth?

Notes for the Teacher—Family structures will dictate the success of this research. Interviews with parents or grandparents may yield the answers to the best of their memories. The best records will be those contained in primary documents created at the time of the event. Parents who have maintained a baby book for the child can help the researcher provide documentation. If several students attempt to answer this question, have them engage in research talk that includes assessment of the quality of the information. For example: "Are the recollections of an adult who was there at the time as credible as the information recorded at the time?"

Mini-Research #15: What is the best-selling children's book in your community? Or in an urban community nearby?

Notes for the Teacher—The difficulty of this research question will vary with the bookstores and the data they keep as well as with the number of bookstores in the community. If your community has only one bookstore, the task may be more easily completed. If the community has several stores that sell books, students may compile data from each of them. This also may be a question for which data is unavailable if those who have the ability to collect the data have not done so.

Mini-Research #16: How many teachers teach in your school building and what is their total number of years' experience?

Notes for the Teacher—This question will be relatively easy to answer since the sources of information are close at hand. However, classroom schedules may make it difficult for students to ask teachers the appropriate questions. In that case, a questionnaire may be designed and distributed to the teachers. Students will need to follow up with those who do not respond to verbally ask the questions. When all the data has been collected, it must be restructured to answer the question.

Primary Documents

One of the first activities concerning primary documents may be to introduce students to a number of different examples. As each document is shared (using a transparency or individual copies) the teacher should model the thinking processes one would use to assess the document and glean information from it. The examples and exercises in this section provide students with opportunities to analyze and examine primary documents to glean information about historic and scientific events. Teachers may wish to use the graphic organizer for the analysis of a primary document as an aid in examining each of the documents presented on the following pages. (See Appendix A for "Looking for Information—Primary Documents.") As a general teaching strategy, students should be introduced to the situation, people, and places involved in creating the document before seeing the document itself. If students have ample prior knowledge about the event, the teacher may spend some time activating that prior knowledge before initiating a discussion of the document. For example, before presenting the diagram Alexander Graham Bell submitted to obtain a patent for his telephone, one might read a short biography of Bell to set the stage. During a read-aloud session, a book such as, Robert M. Quackenbush's *Ahoy! Ahoy! Are You There? A Story of Alexander Graham Bell* (Prentice-Hall, 1981) might be shared and discussed. That humorous account of events in the inventor's life will provide background and a point at which to begin a discussion of Bell before introducing the primary document. After reading the book aloud, students may be encouraged to learn more about the man or to share information they already know. In some cases information that is offered may have to be checked for accuracy. This could provide a stimulus for investigation in the library media center or the primary document may provide verification to some of the doubtful statements. In any case, the "Setting the stage" suggestions for using the primary document are meant to promote discussion and activate the students' schema prior to introducing the primary document.

Document #1—Letter of Credit for Meriwether Lewis

When Meriwether Lewis and William Clark set out to locate a water route west to the Pacific (Lewis and Clark Expedition) they did so with sufficient supplies to last through one leg of the journey. To insure that the members of the expedition would be accorded as much cooperation as possible in obtaining goods and services, President Thomas Jefferson prepared a letter of credit. This letter was given to Lewis, Jefferson's personal secretary, and to Lewis's good friend William Clark who had planned the expedition for several years. A typed transcript of the letter is followed by a copy of the letter itself. This transcription is a secondary source and the letter, because it is an exact copy of the original, is a primary source or document.

Document #1: Transcription

This is a typed transcript of the letter given to Meriwether Lewis by President Thomas Jefferson, dated July 4, 1803. The original is in the National Archives, Washington, D.C.; general records of the United States. The following is as accurate a transcription of the text as can be read from the original document. Readers should note that Jefferson did not begin many sentences with a capital letter and he followed the spelling conventions of the time for words such as "passage" spelling it as "pafsage," "vessel" as "vefsel," and "authorize" as "authorise."

Washington. U.S. of America. July 4, 1803.

Dear Sir

In the journey which you are about to undertake for the discovery of the course and source of the Mississippi and of the most convenient water communication from thence to the Pacific ocean, your party being small, it is to be expected that you will encounter considerable dangers from the Indian inhabitants. should you escape those dangers and reach the Pacific ocean, you may find it imprudent to hazard a return the same way, and be forced to seek a pafsage round by sea in such vefsels as you may find on the Western coast. but you will be without money, without clothes, & other necefsaries; as a sufficient supply cannot be carried with you from hence. your resource in that case can only be in the credit of the US. for which purpose I hereby authorise you to draw on the Secretaries of State, of the Treasury, of War & of the Navy of the US. according as you may find your draughts will be most negociable, for the purpose of obtaining money or necefsaries for yourself & your men: and I solemnly pledge the faith of the United States that these draughts shall be paid punctually at the date they are made payable. I also ask of the Consuls, agents, merchants & citizens of any nation with which we have intercourse or amity to furnish you with those supplies which your necefsities may call for, assuring them of honorable and prompt retribution. and our own Consuls in foreign parts where you may happen to be, are hereby instructed & required to be aiding and assisting to you in whatsoever may be necefsary for procuring your return back to the United States. And to give more entire satisfaction & confidence to those who may be disposed to aid you. I Thomas Jefferson, President of the United States of America, have written this letter of general credit for you with my own hand, and signed it with my name.

Th Jefferson

To Capt. Meriwether Lewis.

Suggested Teaching Activities for Document #1

A. Setting the stage

1. Read aloud: Bowen, Andy Russell. *The Back of the Beyond: A Story about Lewis and Clark.* Carolrhoda, 1996.

2. Read aloud: Petersen, David. *Meriwether Lewis and William Clark: Soldiers, Explorers, and Partners in History.* Children's Press, 1988.

3. Other read-aloud titles: Locate by using the subject heading, "Lewis, Meriwether" or "Clark, William."

4. Read aloud: Kroll, Steven. *Lewis and Clark: Explorers of the American West.* Holiday House, 1994.

5. Other books about the expedition itself may be located by using the subject heading "Lewis and Clark Expedition."

B. Introduction and discussion

1. Provide some general background information about the Lewis and Clark expedition or before this introduction ask students to find out some general information about the expedition. Checking in an encyclopedia will be the most usual method of obtaining general information.

2. Make a transparency of the document or a copy for each student. Share the letter and then discuss these questions.

   a. Why do you think Jefferson wrote this letter?

   b. Do you think it would do the explorers any good? Why or why not?

   c. What information about the expedition can you glean from this letter?

C. Activity suggestions

1. Read about the expedition and create a map tracing the route the explorers took.

2. Prepare a time line to plot the activities of the explorers from the time they left St. Louis to the time they returned again.

3. Put the Lewis and Clark expedition on a time line with other significant events that took place during Jefferson's presidency.

4. Explain the benefits that resulted from Lewis and Clark's expedition.

5. Make a biochart of Meriwether Lewis or William Clark. The chart should provide pictorial representations of major events in the subject's life. (Note: Perhaps it will be of some interest to at least one researcher to discover why Lewis, who was four years younger than Clark, died just three years after returning from the expedition while Clark lived approximately 26 years beyond Lewis's death.)

Document #1

Washington. U.S. of America. July 4. 1803.

Dear Sir

In the journey which you are about to undertake for the discovery of the course and source of the Missisipi and of the most convenient water communication from thence to the Pacific ocean, your party being small, it is to be expected that you will encounter considerable dangers from the Indian inhabitants. should you escape those dangers and reach the Pacific ocean, you may find it imprudent to hazard a return the same way, and be forced to seek a passage round by sea, in such vessels as you may find on the Western coast. but you will be without money, without clothes, & other necessaries; as a sufficient supply cannot be carried with you from hence. your resource in that case can only be in the credit of the U.S. for which purpose I hereby authorise you to draw on the Secretaries of State, of the Treasury, of War & of the Navy of the U.S. according as you may find your draughts will be most negociable, for the purpose of obtaining money or necessaries for yourself & your men: and I solemnly pledge the faith of the United States that these draughts shall be paid punctually at the date they are made payable. I also ask of the Consuls, agents, merchants & citizens of any nation with which we have intercourse or amity, to furnish you with those supplies which your necessities may call for, assuring them of honorable and prompt retribution. and our own Consuls in foreign parts where you may happen to be, are hereby instructed & required to be aiding & assisting to you in whatsoever may be necessary for procuring your return back to the United States. And to give more entire satisfaction & confidence to those who may be disposed to aid you, I Thomas Jefferson, President of the United States of America, have written this letter of general credit for you with my own hand, and signed it with my name.

Th. Jefferson

To Capt. Meriwether Lewis.

Document #2—1880s Census of Dakota Territories

Laura Ingalls was a child in a pioneer family in the Midwest in the second half of the 1800s. After homesteading in Minnesota and Oklahoma Indian Territory for several years, Charles Ingalls and his wife, Caroline, moved their family to the DeSmet, South Dakota, area in the late 1870s. This census of 1880 indicates that Pa Ingalls (Charles) was 44 years old, Ma Ingalls (Caroline) was 40; Mary A. was 15; Laura E. was 13; Caroline C. (Carrie) was nine; and Grace L. was three years old. As an adult, Laura Ingalls authored the widely read *Little House on the Prairie* series, which chronicles her growing-up years in Minnesota, the Oklahoma Indian Territory, and the Dakota Territory.

Document #2: Transcription

This transcription is a typed copy of part of the Dakota Territory Census of 1880; featuring the Ingalls family. The original is in the National Archives, Washington, D.C.; RG 29, Records of the Bureau of the Census.
Entry

	————, Sara R.	W	F	25		wife	1	Housekeeping	
	————, Louis B.	W	M	4/12	Feb.	Son	1	At home	
	Amus, Ellen S.	W	F	35		sister-in-law	1	Teacher	14
2 2	Bradley, George C.	W	M	24			1	Druggist	—
	————, Hattie L.	W	F	22		wife	1	Keeping House	
	————, Clarence E.	W	M	10/12	Aug	son	1	At home	
3 3	Wilmaret, George B.	W	M	38			1	Grocer, retail	√
4 4	Hize, Henry	W	M	26			1	Shoemaker	√
	Hall, Harry W.	W	M	25		partner	1	Works in Shoe Shop	5
5 5	Barker, Charles P.	W	M	38			1	Grocer, retail	3
	————, Elizabeth L.	W	F	30		Wife	1	Keeping House	
	————, Frederick A.	W	M	2		Son	1	At Home	
	————, Earl	W	M	4/12	Feb	Son	1	At Home	
	Dutton, Carrie	W	F	15		Servant	1	Servant	√
6 6	Ferguson, George M.	W	M	29			1	Butcher	√
7 7	Hawthorn, Edelbert M.	W	M	39			1	Grocer, retail	
	————, Frank L.	W	F	23		Son	1	Grocer, retail	
8 8	Woodruff, Jerome	W	M	50			1	Dealer in Feed	—
	————, Merrill J.	W	M	23		Son	1	Farm Laborer	
9 9	Gore, Frank E.	W	M	22			1	Retail Grocer	3
	Gibson, Thomas	W	M	32		Lodger	1	Farmer	—
10 10	Kennedy, David A.	W	M	50			1	Dealer. Agrl. Implements	3
11 11	Fuller, Charlain S.G.	W	M	30			1	Dealer Hardware	—
	————, Gerald C.R.	W	M	30		Brother	1	Dealer Agrl. Implements	—
	Hopp, Jacob W.	W	M	22		Lodger	1	Printer	√
12 12	Barnes, Visscher F.	W	M	29			1	Lawyer	√
13 13	Ingalls, Charles P.	W	M	44			1	Farmer	
	————, Caroline L.	W	F	40		Wife	1	Keeping House	
	————, Mary A.	W	F	15		Daughter	1	Help in keeping house	
	————, Laura E.	W	F	13		Daughter	1	Help in keeping house	
	————, Caroline C.	W	F	9		Daughter	1		
	————, Grace L.	W	F	3		Daughter	1		
14	Masters, George E.	W	M	27			1	1 Clerk in Store	
	————, Margaret	W	F	22		Wife	1	1 House Keeper	1
	————, George E. Jr.	W	M	4/12	April	Son	1		
14 14	Crook, William H.	W	M	22			1	Tinsmith	
	Tinkham, Charles H.	W	M	26		Boarder	1	Cabinet Maker	
15 15	McKee, James W.	W	M	30			1	Dealer in Drygoods	4
	————, Martha E.	W	F	30		Wife	1	Keeping house	
	————, Mary E.	W	F	8		Daughter	1		
16 16	Drake, Hobart A.	W	M	25			1	Farmer	√
17 18	Clayson, Chaucey L.	W	M	31			1	Dealer Drygoods	—

Suggested Teaching Activities for Document #2

A. Setting the stage
   1. Read aloud: Anderson, William. *Laura Ingalls Wilder: A Biography.* HarperCollins, 1992.
   2. Read aloud: Giff, Patricia Reilly. *Growing Up in the Little House.* Viking Kestrel, 1987.
   3. Read one of the *Little House* books. The book that chronicles events during the period of the census would have been *The Long Winter* by Laura Ingalls Wilder, illustrated by Garth Williams (Harper, 1940; 1953). Almanzo Wilder makes a dangerous trip to secure wheat to save the village from starvation during the terrible winter of 1880-'81. When trains with food are unable to make it over the snow-covered tracks, the Ingalls family has to use a coffee grinder to grind wheat into flour. In the next book, *Little Town on the Prairie* (Harper, 1941; 1953), Laura, age 15, receives a certificate to teach school.
   4. Watch the video *Meet the Newbery Author: Laura Ingalls Wilder,* produced by American School Publishers (distributed by DLM), n.d.
B. Introduction and discussion
   1. Provide general background about Laura and her family. Give researchers the date of Laura's birth (1867). That fact alone will help date Document #2 as a copy of the 1880 census. Censuses are taken every ten years and would have been taken in 1870, 1880, and 1890.
   2. Make a transparency of the document or a copy for each student. Share the census record and attempt to figure out what each column means.

   Column 1: (example: 13 13) This probably indicates the house, lot, or plot of land where the residence is located.

   Column 2: (example: Ingalls, Charles P.) Name at the address, probably the head of the household. A dash indicates that the last name is the same as the one above, a member of the same family.

   Column 3: (example: W) This indicates that the person on the census was "white." The designation for a non-white person is unknown since none of the people listed on this page is other than white.

   Column 4: (example: F or M) Indicates female or male. One mistake was made. In the row "7 7" a child, "Frank L." is listed as "F" but in one of the next columns is called "son." Clearly, one or the other is in error.

   Column 5: (example: 44) This column indicates the age of the person listed on the census.

   Column 6: (example: wife) Indicates the relationship to the head of the household. In most cases it is *wife, daughter,* or *son.* But some are termed *servant, boarder,* or *partner.*

   Column 7: (example: farmer) Indicates occupation. When a child was 15 or so, an occupation was listed such as helping with housekeeping or shoemaker, farmer, printer. Most adult females are listed as *Keeping House* while males have an occupation such as a farmer or store clerk.

Column 8: (example: √ or 4) The document does not indicate the meaning of this column.

    a. What can you determine about the Ingalls family from this document?

    b. In one resource, this document was cited as a copy of the census from the 1870s. How can one determine that the citation was inaccurate? Note: Many documents verify that Laura Ingalls Wilder was born in 1867. In 1870 she would have been just three years old; and in 1880 she would have been 13 as this document states. In addition, other documentation verifies that the family was not living in the Dakotas at the time of the 1870 census.

3. What significant information can you determine from this document?

    a. What do you already know about the Ingalls family that would fit with this document?

    b. How long had they lived in this area?

    c. What book recounts Laura's memory of this period?

    d. Are there any other names on this census that you recognize?

C. Activity suggestions

1. Locate general information about the population of the Dakotas during this period. This census shows that the residents were "W" (white): Is that true for the rest of the Dakotas? Note: Keep in mind that the Dakotas were populated by Native Americans long before white settlers arrived. A special census of the Creek Nation was conducted in 1832 and of the Cherokee Nation in 1834, but most Native Americans were not counted on the nation's census until 1860, which listed Native Americans living among the general population. Those living on reservations were counted in yearly federal censuses for most of the years between 1855 and 1940. The 1870 census, the first one taken after the Civil War, was also the first that listed African-Americans by name. Previously African-Americans had been counted as "free Negroes" and earlier they had not been counted at all.

2. Visit an historical library in your area and locate a census listing one of your ancestral families.

Document #2

1	1	Darroll Thomas	W M 3.		1		Clerk District Court	
		Dana R.	W F 25	wife	1		House Keeping	
		Lewis B	W M 4/12 Feb	Son	1		At home	
		Truex Ellen J.	W F 35	Sister in law	1		Teacher	4
2	2	Bradley George C.	W M 24		1		Druggist	—
		Hattie L.	W F 22	wife	1		Keeping House	
		Clarence E.	W M 1/12 Aug	Son	1		At home	
3	3	Wilmarth George B.	W M 38		1		Grocer, retail	✓
4	4	King Henry	W M 26		1		Shoemaker	✓
		Hall Harry W.	W M 25	partner	1		Works in Shoe Shop	5
5	5	Barker Charles P.	W M 35		1		Grocer, retail	3
		Elizabeth T.	W F 30	wife	1		Keeping House	
		Frederick A.	W M 2	Son	1		At Home	
		Earl	W M 4/12 Feb	Son	1		At Home	
		Dutton Carrie	W F 15	Servant	1		Servant	✓
6	6	Ferguson George M	W M 29		1		Butcher	
7	7	Hawthorn Edelbert M.	W M 39		1		Grocer, retail	
		Frank L	W F 33	Son	1		Grocer retail	✓
8	8	Woodruff Jerome	W M 50		1		Dealer in field	—
		Merrell J.	W M 23	Son	1		Farm laborer	✓
9	9	Gore Frank L	W M 22		1		Retail Grocer	3
		Gibson Thomas	W M 32	Lodger	1		Farmer	—
10	10	Kennedy David A.	W M 50		1		Dealer Agl Impl	3
11	11	Fuller Charles G.	W M 30		1		Dealer Hardware	—
		Gerald C R	W M 30	Brother	1		Dealer Agl Impl	—
		Hopp, Jacob W.	W M 22	Lodger	1		Printer	✓
12	12	Barnes Fletcher T	W M 29		1		Lawyer	✓
13	13	Ingalls Charles P.	W M 44		1		Farmer	✓
		Caroline L.	W F 41	wife	1		Keeping House	
		Mary A.	W F 15	Daughter	1		Help in Keeping House	
		Laura E.	W F 13	Daughter	1		Help in Keeping House	
		Caroline C.	W F 9	Daughter	1			
		Grace L.	W F 3	Daughter	1			
	14	Master George E.	W M 27			1	1	Clerk in Store	✓
		Margaret	W F 23	wife		1	1	House Keeper	1
		George E. jr	W M 4/12 April	Son	1			
14	14	Crook William H	W M 22		1		Tinsmith	
		Tinkham Charles H.	W M 26	Brother	1	1	Cabinet maker	
15	15	McKee James W	W M 30		1		Dealer in Organs	4
		Martha E.	W F 30	wife	1		Keeping House	
		Mary E.	W F 8	Daughter	1			
16	16	Drake Herbert A	W M 25		1		Farmer	✓
17	18	Clauson Chauss L	W M 21		1			—

Document #3 — Letter Signed by Frederick Douglass

Frederick Douglass was born a slave in Maryland about February 1817. During his life he became an active abolitionist. As a young man he was sent to Baltimore to work in the shipyards. His master's wife had taught him the letters of the alphabet and he continued to learn words and letters by tracing the letters on the prows of ships. At age 21 he used seaman's papers supplied by a free black to escape to Massachusetts. Later, he became involved in the anti-slavery movement. He began to give speeches stemming from reminiscences of slave life and to call for slavery's immediate abolition. As his speaking ability became more polished, many doubted that he actually had been a slave. As proof he risked re-enslavement by publishing his *Narrative of the Life of Frederick Douglass* (later titled: *Life and Times of Frederick Douglass*). In 1847, after two years spent in Britain speaking against slavery, some British friends purchased his legal freedom for 150 pounds. He left London and returned to the United States to continue the fight against slavery. Douglass encouraged Blacks to join the Union Army and assisted in their recruitment. Frederick Douglass served as Assistant Secretary of the Santo Domingo Commission in 1871, Marshall from 1877 to 1881, Recorder of Deeds in Washington, D.C., from 1881 to 1886, and as U.S. Minister to Haiti from 1889 to 1891.

Douglass's later years were devoted to being an advocate for his people and for all who were not being treated fairly. Douglass felt Blacks must speak out to make others aware of what was happening. Douglass felt that he had to draw attention to the rampant lynchings that were taking place in the South in the 1890s. The others who signed the letter with Douglass cannot be located in any of several general encyclopedias checked. Douglass continued to work for reform until the day he died, February 20, 1895, when he collapsed after attending a women's suffrage meeting.

Document #3: Transcription

This typed transcription is of a letter on United States Senate letterhead (undated but determined to be February, 1893) from Frederick Douglass, Francis J. Grimke, Walter H. Brooks, and Mary Church Terrell. The original is in the National Archives, Washington, D.C.; RG 90, Records of the United States Senate.

Frederick Douglass was an outspoken critic of the mob lynchings that took place in the Southern States.

United States Senate,
WASHINGTON, D.C., , 189 .

The undersigned citizens of the United States pray the Hon.
Senate of the United States to instruct the Judiciary
Committee of the Senate to grant a hearing of a statement
in respect to the lawless outrages committed in some of the
Southern States upon persons accused of crime, but who
are denied the ordinary means of establishing their
innocence by due process of law.

Frederick Douglass
Francis J. Grimke
Walter H. Brooks
Mary Church Terrell

Suggested Teaching Activities for Document #3

A. Setting the stage
   1. Read aloud: McKissack, Patricia and Fredrick McKissack. *Frederick Douglass: Leader Against Slavery.* Enslow, 1991.
   2. Read aloud: Adler, David A. *A Picture Book of Frederick Douglass.* Illustrated by Samuel Byrd.
   3. Investigate and locate information about Frederick Douglass in an encyclopedia. Using the keyword search function of CD-ROM encyclopedias will be an effective way to obtain basic information about Douglass.
B. Introduction and discussion
   1. Discuss general information about Douglass and list information that is known about him.
   2. Make a transparency of the document or a copy for each student. Share the letter and then discuss these questions.
      a. What is the date of this document? (Note: Douglass died in 1895 and even though the letter is not dated, the printing indicates that the year would have been at least 1890.)
      b. What events prompted the writing of this letter?
      c. Why do you think Douglass felt he should write this letter?
      d. Do you think the letter had any effect on what events continued or did not continue?
      e. What questions do you have because of this document?

C. Activity suggestions
1. Search for answers to some of the questions raised by the document.
2. Research what life was like in the United States during the early 1890s.
3. Identify Douglass's major accomplishments and put them on a time line. Add other significant events in the United States history to the time line to put Douglass's accomplishments in perspective.
4. Research and locate names of some of Douglass's contemporaries. Who were some significant contributors to history that Douglass might have known?
5. Research and confirm the relationships between Douglass and some of the contemporaries identified in item #4.

Document #3

United States Senate,

WASHINGTON, D. C.,   , 189 .

The undersigned citizens of the
United States pray the Hon. Senate
of the United States to instruct
the Judiciary Committee of the
Senate to grant a hearing of
a statement in respect to the
lawless outrages committed
in some of the Southern States
upon persons accused of
crime, but who are denied
the ordinary means of establishing their innocence by due
process of law,

                    Frederick Douglass
                    Francis J. Grimké
                    Walter H. Brooks
                    Mary Church Terrell.

Document #4—Notes of Special Inquiry Held at Ellis Island, 1903

From the turn of the century until Ellis Island was shut down as an immigrant processing center in 1954, thousands of immigrants passed through that first stopping point. Upon arriving at Ellis Island, immigrants were inspected by guards and doctors. Some days saw the arrival of more than 16,000 people. Most could not speak English and had to be questioned through an interpreter. If the person were found to have a "defect" such as: deafness, heart problems, mental illness, lameness, or trachoma (an eye disease), the person's coat was marked with chalk and he or she was separated from the other immigrants. Sometimes a child would be disallowed and parents had to decide whether one parent would return to their homeland with the child or send the youngster alone. Passage through Ellis Island often took up to four hours. About two of every hundred were sent back. During processing many immigrants received new names: for example, Mueller might become Miller, Oeschger might become Esker, and Simonov might become Simon.

When immigrants arrived in the United States they were expected to have enough money to keep themselves or to have relatives in this country who could support them. Immigrants were not allowed to enter the country to take a job from a citizen. This was referred to as Alien Contract Labor Law.

Document #4: Analysis

This is a typed record of inquiry held at Ellis Island by the Third Board of Inquiry, dated October 2, 1903. The original document is in the National Archives, Washington, D.C. While a transcript is not necessary, some general information may help teachers prepare strategies for the student lesson. From the document one can deduce that Friedrich Unch came to the United States and landed at Ellis Island October 1, 1903. A native of Hungary, 25 years old, he was married with a wife and child in Hungary. He arrived aboard the SS Kronprinz Wilhelm. His passage had been paid for by Unch's father. At home Friedrich Unch was a farmer. He had been in the United States previously and had stayed for three years, however, he had returned home in 1888. He was overheard to have referred to a promise of work at $1.50 per day, as arranged by a cousin, Andreas Schneider in Newcastle, Pennsylvania. On the following day three inspectors held an inquiry at 9:30 A.M. Mr. Semsey, chairman, served as the interpreter. The secretary, C.E. Lovejoy, was also present as was Mr. Lee, the third inspector who seemed to take the lead in the inquiry. Mr. Lee led Friedrich Unch to discuss the letter from his cousin. The foreman had already assured Unch's cousin that Unch could be a helper at the tin mine and earn $1.50 per day. From Friedrich Unch's statements it was clear to the inspectors that Unch had been induced to come to the United States by the promise of work. Since the Alien Contract Labor Law prohibits aliens from entering the United States to take a job from a citizen, Unch was deported to his homeland.

Suggested Teaching Activities for Document #4

A. Setting the stage
   1. Share the information from the section Document #4: Analysis.
   2. Discuss the concept of immigration.
   3. Discuss the Alien Contract Labor Law and what it means.
   4. Read aloud: Jacobs, William Jay. *Ellis Island: New Hope in a New Land*. Illustrated with photographs. Scribner's, 1990.
   5. Read aloud: Siegel, Beatrice. *Sam Ellis's Island*. Four Winds, 1985.
   6. Read aloud: Levine, Ellen. *If Your Name Was Changed at Ellis Island*. Illustrated by Wayne Parmenter. Scholastic, 1993.

B. Introduction and discussion
   1. Make a collaborative list of facts known about Ellis Island. Discuss why people would have entered the United States at the turn of the century.
   2. Discuss the meanings of the words *alien*, *deported*, *immigration*, *passage*, *native*, *destination*, *unanimously*, *violation*, *foreman*, *engaged*, *inducement*, *sworn*, and *testified*.
   3. Make a transparency of the document or a copy for each student. Ask each student to read the document (buddy-read if necessary or read aloud as students follow along).
      a. Do you think Friedrich Unch had any idea of the Alien Contract Labor Law?
      b. Do you think this law is still in effect today?
      c. Why do you think the law was passed?
      d. Do you think it is wise to exclude immigrants from prearranging work before they arrive in the United States? Note: Consider the effect on the job situation for citizens or residents already here and the strain on family and friends if work is not guaranteed. What happens if the immigrant can't get a job?

C. Activity suggestions
   1. Write a definition of the Alien Contract Labor Law.
   2. Investigate immigration laws in effect today. (Check the Internet for the *Immigration Library* and the *Immigration Naturalization Service*.)
   3. Read one of Joan Lowery Nixon's Ellis Island series books such as: *Land of Hope* (Bantam, 1992), or *Land of Promise* (Bantam, 1993).

Document #4

THIRD BOARD:

    At a Special Inquiry, held at Ellis Island, N.Y., Oct. 2, 1903.

Present: Messrs. Semsey (Chairman) Hinkley and Lee, Inspectors.

Board convened at 9:30 a.m.   C. E. Lovejoy, Secretary.

Mr. Semsey, Interpreter.

Page 79-L
Case of UNCH, Friedrich, m, 25, German-Hungary, ex ss "Kronprinz
Wilhelm" Oct. 1, 1903. "C.L.Admitted to have work prepared by cousin
at $1.50 per day". Grgurevich, Insp.
Alien, sworn, testified:
    I am 25 years of age; native of Hungary, wife and one child
in Hungary; my father, at home, paid my passage to America; farmer;
I was three years in America before and left here in 1888. I am
going to my cousin, Andreas Schneider, Newcastle, Pa. (Exhibits R.R.
ticket to destination and $5.00)
Mr. Lee:
Q   When did you hear from your cousin? A One month ago. I can
    read and write. I read the letter myself.
Mr. Semsey:
Q   Tell the Board what was in that letter in regard to your com-
    ing to America? A He wrote me that he is working in a tin
    factory and if I will come to America he is going to try and
    get work for me over there where he is working.
Mr. Lee:
Q   Did you say, out on the line, when you were registered, that
    you had work prepared for you by your cousin at $1.50 per day?
    A I said I am going to get $1.50 a day.
Q   Did the letter state that to you? A He wrote to me that I
    am going to be a helper to him and I am going to receive $1.50
    a day.
Q   You are positive about that statement; that he stated you were
    going to be a helper to him and get $1.50 a day? A He said
    that I am going to be a helper to him and that the company will
    pay me $1.50 a day.
Q   Did he say in the letter that he had spoken to the foreman or
    boss and engaged that work for you? A He wrote that he had
    spoken with the foreman and the foreman answered him that when
    I come here he is going to give me work.
Q   Is that what induced you to come here at this time? A Yes.
Q   Would you have come if you had not had that inducement from
    your cousin? A No.
Mr. Lee:
    Move to exclude him as coming in violation of the Alien Con-
tract Labor Law and also the Law of March 3, 1903.
Mr. Hinkley:
    I second the motion.
Chairman:
    The alien immigrant is unanimously excluded as coming in viola-
tion of the Alien Contract Labor Law and ordered deported.

    Alien informed of exclusion and right of appeal.

No appeal. Deported 10/7·03 S.S. "Fred. der Grosse"

Document #5—Driver's Contract

Many school districts have buses to transport students to and from school. This document details a school bus agreement entered into on August 8, 1924, between I.E. Lang, President of the Board of Directors of the Independent School District of Lamont in Madison Township, Buchanan County, Iowa and P.J. Hansen of (unnamed) Township, (unnamed) County, Iowa. The agreement contracted Hansen to provide transportation for school children on "Route No. 13" to the Lamont Cons. School in Lamont each day that school was in session during the school year beginning August 25, 1924. To complete his contract, Hansen was to comply with 12 points relating to the transportation. For his services Hansen was to be paid $35.50 per month.

Document #5: Analysis

The first condition of this contract specifies that Hansen will "furnish a safe, strong team with proper harness." Reading further, one can determine that the driver (Hansen) "will not allow the school wagons to be used for any other purpose and report any damage to hacks to the Superintendent." And later in the document there is mention of the fact that "A safe strong wagon complete, is to be furnished by Board of Directors." Not stated in the contract but said to be common practice based on interviews with Hansen's children is the fact that most drivers also provided bales of straw or hay placed in the wagon to create make-shift bench seats for the pupils being transported. Item #2 specifies that the driver was to furnish "comfortable blankets and robes, sufficient for the best protection of the pupils while on the road." Several conditions are set to insure that the Board of Directors receives its money's worth. For example, if the route is shortened during the school year, the monthly payment will be reduced by $2.50 per mile. Conversely, if the number of miles is increased, the amount of pay will increase by an equal amount. If, however, the driver is frequently late in delivering the children to school in the morning or late in starting the trip to their homes after school, the driver is to be fined $1.00 for each failure except for unavoidable reasons. The Board of Directors also held back one-half of the first month's pay until the contract was satisfied, to insure that the driver completed the school year or gave ample notice.

Suggested Teaching Activities for Document #5

A. Setting the stage
   1. Survey students to determine how each gets to school. How many ride city buses? How many walk? How many ride school buses? How many are driven to school by family members? Create a summary graph or chart showing the results of the survey.
   2. Share Donald Crews's book *School Bus* (Greenwillow, 1984). The book shows some dramatic views of the traditional yellow school bus and will set the stage for activities and discussion.
B. Introduction and discussion
   1. Initiate discussion about how children might have arrived at school in earlier days, before automobiles were common.
   2. Collect examples of ways students got to school by finding descriptions

in books such as those by Laura Ingalls Wilder and others who write school stories, such as Beverly Cleary, Carolyn Haywood, and Barbara Parks.

3. Make a copy of the document for each student. Ask students to read the contract (with a buddy or read aloud) then pose these questions:
   a. What is the date of this document?
   b. What does this contract mean?
   c. Who entered into this contract? What was each party in this contract supposed to do?
   d. Does this question make you wonder about any other aspects of getting to school? Note: Some common questions generated by the use of this document include, what did children sit on in the wagon? Did they go to school when it was raining? Snowing? What happened if they got to school and the horses couldn't get through the snow to take them home?

C. Activity suggestions
   1. Use the figures in the contract to create mathematical problems. For example: How much money would Hansen have earned during the term of the contract? If Hansen's contract were increased or decreased by $2.50 for each mile added or removed from the route, estimate the number of miles on the established route ($35 \div \$2.50 = 14$ miles).
   2. Locate neighbors and relatives who might have attended school in 1924. Interview them concerning how they might have gotten to school and answer some of the questions generated in section B. The people were born between the years 1907 and 1919. Those born in 1919 would have been five-year-olds in 1924 and those born in 1907 would have been 17.
   3. Investigate driver's contracts in your school district. Are drivers required to sign individual contracts? Is there a master contract? How does the contract compare to the 1924 document?

Document #5

State of Iowa Form 61

(Under provision of Section 2794-a School Laws of Iowa)

DRIVER'S CONTRACT
(CONSOLIDATED SCHOOL DISTRICT)

THIS AGREEMENT, Made and entered into by and between .....I..E..Lang.............. President of the Board of Directors of the Independent School District of ......Lamont............ in ..Madison....... Township ..Buchanan...... County, Iowa, and .......P..J..Hansen........... of .... Township, ... County, Iowa.

Said ..P.J?.Hansen................. covenants and agrees to transport the children of Route No..13 to the ..Lamont.Cons........ School in ..Lamont........... each day that school is in session during the school year beginning ...Aug..25,1924..... Said......P.J.Hansen.............. further agrees to comply with the following conditions:

1. He will furnish a safe, strong team with proper harness.
2. He will furnish comfortable blankets and robes, sufficient for the best protection of the pupils while on the road.
3. He will collect the pupils by driving over the route each morning as directed by the board, in time to convey the pupils to school so as to arrive at the school building not earlier than ..8:45.... o'clock a. m. or later than ..9:10... a. m., waiting not longer than ..three ..(3).... minutes and blowing a whistle, or some other suitable signal, at each house.
4. He will return the pupils to their homes, leaving the school house at ..3:30......p. m., or later, as the board may determine.
5. He will personally drive and manage the team, or provide a suitable driver satisfactory to the board, who will comply with all the conditions of this contract.
6. He will refrain from the use of profane language in the presence of the pupils.
7. He will not use tobacco in any form during the time he is conveying the pupils to and from school.
8. He will avoid fast driving and racing with other teams and stop before crossing the railroad and be sure that no train is coming and that it is safe and clear before attempting to cross.
9. He will keep order among the pupils and report any improper conduct to the Superintendent.
10. He will not allow the school wagons to be used for any other purpose, and report any damage to hacks to the Superintendent.
11. Should a driver frequently arrive at the schoolhouse late in the morning or be late to start to return the pupils to their homes, unless for unavoidable reasons, he shall be fined the sum of $1.00 for each failure.
12. There will be a reduction made pro rata from the above stated salary for each day on which there is no school during the regular school month. (Balance of conditions on back of this contract.)

In consideration of the said services the said ......I.E..Lang.............., President of the Board, in behalf of the Independent School District of ....Lamont...................., hereby agrees to pay the said .....P..J..Hansen............. the sum of .$35.50.......... dollars per month, excepting it is herein agreed that the board shall retain one-half of the first month's wages until the close of the term of service of .......P..J..Hansen............ to insure the faithful performance of the terms of this contract. The Board of Directors reserves the right to terminate this contract at any time.

The board reserves the right to change the route when they consider it necessary for the best interests of the patrons. In case of change ..$2.50.......... per month will be added for each additional mile added to the route. When the route is shortened $2.50.... per month will be deducted for each mile taken from the route.

A safe strong wagon complete, is to be furnished by ....Board.of.Directors...................
....

IN TESTIMONY WHEREOF we have hereunto subscribed our names this .....8th.............. day of .....Aug........., 1924...

....
President

....
Driver

Document #6—Prairie Land Advertisement

During the 1870s millions of acres in the middle of the United States were opened for sale and homesteading. Enterprising companies acquired vast acreages and then offered them for sale. This was the same era in which Charles and Caroline Ingalls took their family to Indian Territory (Oklahoma) to settle. In 1871, when the government threatened to evict the Ingalls because they were on Indian land, Pa and Ma Ingalls packed their family in such haste that they left a plow in the field and headed back to the Minnesota area they had left. The government concern was not so much that the Ingalls were encroaching on Indian land as that the Ingalls had not followed government procedure for obtaining the land. The Homestead Act was passed by the U.S. Congress in 1862 and granted 160 acres of public land in the West, often Indian lands that the government had obtained by forcing Indians off, as a Homestead to "any person who is the head of a family, or who has arrived at the age of twenty-one years, and is a citizen of the United States, or who shall have filed his declaration of intention to become such." The homesteader had to pay only a small filing fee, live on the land for 5 years, and make certain improvements in order to receive clear title. The Homestead Act remained in effect with several modifications until it was repealed in 1977. However, most of the lands were gone by 1900 when about 600,000 farmers had received clear title to an estimated 80 million acres.

The success of the Homestead Act is not clear. While many farmers obtained virtually free land and the government accomplished its objective of distributing the vast lands on the Western frontier, and stemming the spread of slavery (basically the western states were declared "free states"), others questioned the act's success. Better lands were gobbled up by the railroads and by speculators who then forced settlers to buy from them or accept the poorer government lands. That is the situation the accompanying document advertises.

Document #6: Analysis

This advertisement seems to verify what we know about the Homestead Act and the fact that railroads procured the better lands then offered them for sale. The advertisement offers "The best prairie lands in Iowa and Nebraska" and suggests "Products will pay for land and improvements," the company is offering "Large discounts for cash," and those who wish to obtain the terms of the advertisement including the reduced fare and freight charges must "Buy before July 1st, 1875." The selling company is the Burlington & Missouri River Railroad Company. Their terms include ten years of credit at a low price and six per cent interest. Purchasers are enticed by the statements that "Only the interest payment down" is necessary and that "Payments on (the) principal begin the fourth year." The railroad offers to deduct from the first payment the cost of tickets to explore any land bought within 90 days from the date of the ticket. Land purchasers could buy half-fare tickets for family members to travel to their new home. Potential buyers were also promised low freights for household goods and farm tools and circulars with "full information on every location, will be sent free to every applicant." Large sectional maps of Iowa and Nebraska were offered at 30 cents each. Those interested were to contact the land commissioner of the B & M R.R. For Nebraska lands, the offices were in Lincoln, Nebraska; and for Iowa lands, in Burlington, Iowa.

Suggested Teaching Activities for Document #6

A. Setting the stage
1. Discuss information about the Homestead Act of 1862. In Wilder's *The Long Winter* (Harper, 1940) by Laura Ingalls Wilder, Laura discusses the regulations and abuses of the Homestead Act. Read aloud the section from page 98, "Royal had to agree that not even Mother could beat Almanzo at making pancakes" to page 100, "if he could stick it out on these prairies and raise crops for four years more he would have his own farm." In *Little Town on the Prairie* (Harper, 1941) Laura talks about the effect of the Homestead Act on families. Read aloud the section from page 49, "The boys and girls that Laura had met . . ." to page 50, "All the new settlers were beginning where Pa had begun a year ago."
2. Make a collaborative list of some of the rules of the Homestead Act and ways some people got around the act and obtained land for themselves. Discuss how students think railroads could have obtained the best land. Note: Definitive information about why railroads could obtain the best lands seems to be unavailable. One may speculate that since railroads were often the first to enter the West they might have had the opportunity to identify and purchase the better lands.

B. Introduction and discussion
1. Make a transparency of the advertisement and then ask the following questions.
   a. Who is the advertiser?
   b. What is the date of the advertisement? Although there is not a date of distribution, one can date the advertisement as prior to July 1, 1875, and probably after the Homestead Act of 1862.
   c. Why would settlers want to purchase these lands rather than attempt to secure lands from the federal government through the Homestead Act?
   d. How do you suppose the railroad obtained these lands?
   e. Does this advertisement generate any other questions that are not answered by the document?

C. Activity suggestions
1. Find references to the Homestead Act in other books and share them in class. (Wilder's books contain no other references than the two listed in section A; however, readers might use the library media center's catalog to locate books set in the 1860s through the 1880s.)
2. Prepare a time line showing the dates of the Homestead Act, the date of the advertisement, and the dates that Iowa and Nebraska gained statehood.
3. Figure out how much money a purchaser of 160 acres of land for $500 would pay in interest the first year. Then figure how much the purchaser would have paid at the end of four years when the principal payments begin. Explain the concepts of interest and principal.

Document # 6

Documents #7 and #8—Birth Certificates; dated April 24, 1973

These two documents are the fronts and backs of two birth certificates. Together they will demonstrate that we can only interpret information to which we have access. These two documents are the birth certificates of twin males born in 1973. The first birth certificate is that of Steven John Miller born at 4:39 A.M., April 24, 1973, at Mercy Hospital in Cedar Rapids, Iowa. The second certificate is that of his twin brother Matthew John Miller born six minutes later at 4:45 A.M.

Documents #7 and #8: Analysis

The goal for presenting these two documents is to emphasize that with each new document or piece of paper connected to an event there is the potential for gaining additional information. After the first birth certificate is examined and as much information gleaned as possible, the second birth certificate should be examined and information gleaned from it. The most important questions to ask, after the second birth certificate is revealed, are "What additional information do we now know about Steven?" and "What do we know about Matthew that we would not have known without the birth certificate of Steven?"

Suggested Teaching Activities for Documents #7 and #8

A. Setting the stage
   1. Discuss how births are recorded and registered in county courthouses. Hospitals usually present a certificate of birth and when the birth is registered with the county or state, the government issues a document certifying that the birth has been registered.
   2. Suggest that students may wish to look up their own birth certificates to see what they look like.
B. Introduction and discussion
   1. Make a transparency of Steven's birth certificate. Discuss and list information that can be gleaned from the front and back of the document.
      a. Baby born at 4:39 A.M., April 24, 1973, a Tuesday.
      b. Baby was a male.
      c. Baby weighed 5 pounds and 8 ounces.
      d. Baby was 19 inches long.
      e. Baby was born in Mercy Hospital in Cedar Rapids, Iowa.
      f. An official copy of the birth can be obtained from the Iowa State Department of Health in Des Moines, Iowa.
      g. Baby was named Steven John Miller.
      h. Parents of the baby were Catherine Simons Miller and John Miller.
   2. After discussing the first birth certificate introduce a transparency of the second birth certificate (Matthew's) and discuss it. Usually students will recognize that the second birth certificate is similar to the first. Most will figure out that the two babies are twins. Allow that comment to lead to some additional critical thinking. Ask:
      a. If we now discover a second birth certificate, how do we know that

there is not a third birth certificate, or a fourth?

    b. Without knowing whether there is additional information such as another birth certificate that we don't have, what can we say about these two babies?

        (1) The two are brothers.

        (2) The two babies are siblings born as part of a multiple birth.

        (3) Steven was almost two pounds heavier and three inches longer than Matthew.

3. Now list the information that we know about Matthew.

    a. Baby born at 4:45 A.M. on April 24, 1973, a Tuesday.

    b. Baby was a male.

    c. Baby weighed 3 pounds and 10 ounces.

    d. Baby was 16 inches long.

    e. Baby was born in Mercy Hospital in Cedar Rapids, Iowa.

    f. An official copy of the birth can be obtained from the Iowa State Department of Health in Des Moines, Iowa.

    g. Baby was named Matthew John Miller.

    h. Parents of the baby were Catherine Simons Miller and John Miller.

    i. Matthew was born six minutes after his brother was born.

    j. Matthew has a brother named Steven.

4. Additional information we now know about Steven.

    a. Steven was born six minutes before a brother.

    b. Steven has a brother named Matthew.

5. What questions do we have after examining these certificates?

C. Activity suggestions

1. List the questions generated by the discussion in section B.

2. For each question discuss how one would determine the answers. Since these certificates are for children not in your immediate vicinity, locating answers will be more difficult; however, if they were for family members, researchers would have a legitimate reason to request documents from the state. One question that is generally asked, especially because of the three pounds 10 ounce weight of the second baby, is whether or not both children lived. In a real situation a state-level search for a death certificate would determine that fact. It would be fairly easy to discover if a death certificate were filed in the first month or two. After that a search becomes more difficult because it would not have a definable time span. (In fact, both children have grown to adulthood). Other questions should be analyzed in terms of where and how answers to the questions could be obtained.

Document # 7

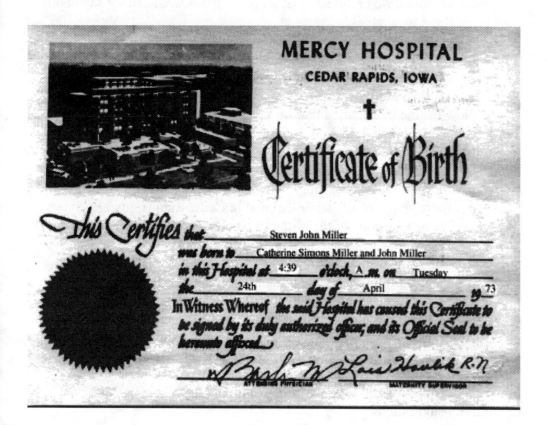

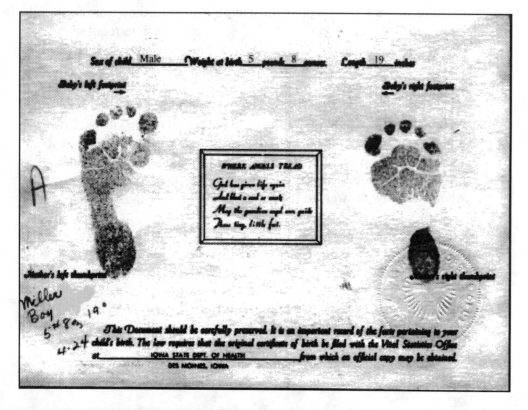

Research Strategies for Moving Beyond Reporting

Document # 8

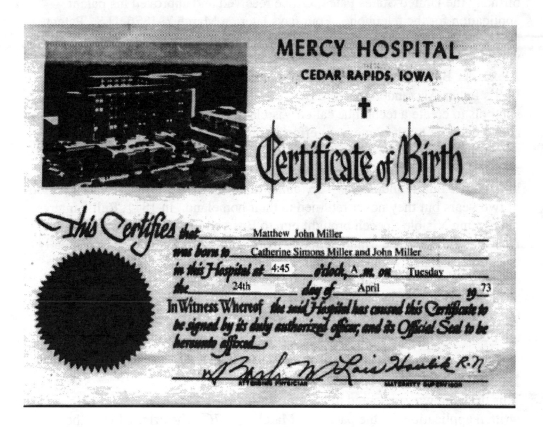

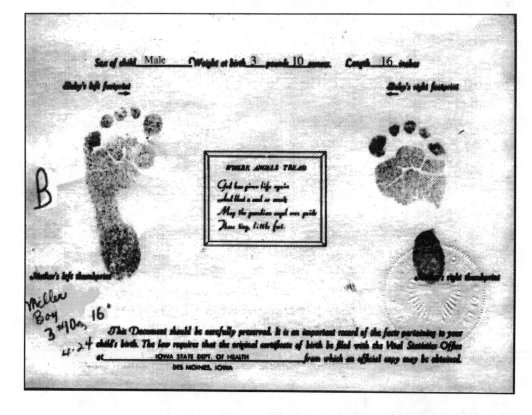

Document # 9—Patent Application of A. Graham Bell

Alexander Graham Bell was born March 3, 1847, in Scotland. On his 29th birthday the United States Patent Office received and approved his patent application for the telephone. Four days later on March 7, 1876, U.S. Patent No. 174,465 for the telephone was granted to Bell. Alexander Graham Bell was the namesake of both his father and grandfather who were both named Alexander Bell. Both were involved with the study and treatment of the deaf. Bell's father Alexander Melville Bell, developed the system of writing speech symbols to create a technique called Visible Speech. At the age of 11, Bell added Graham to his name in an effort to distinguish himself from his father and grandfather. In 1870, the 23-year-old Bell and his parents sailed to North America and settled in Ontario, Canada, to escape disease that had already killed other family members. The family intended to stay only for a trial period of two years but they never returned to their homeland. In 1871, Bell's interest in teaching Visible Speech brought him to Boston to teach at the School of the Deaf (later the Horace Mann School). Through his work there Bell eventually became associated with Helen Keller who remained a lifelong friend. He arranged for tutors for her and became her mentor. Alexander Graham Bell became very involved in the education of the deaf. His interest was influenced by the deafness of his mother and his wife, Mabel. His invention of the telephone resulted from his work with musical and vocal sounds.

Document #9: Analysis

This drawing was presented to the United States Patent Office along with a written application for the patent on March 3, 1876. The original is in the National Archives, Washington, D.C.; RG 241. The drawing refers to the schematic drawing as being presented by "A.G. Bell" and is the second of two sheets, the first being the written application. The drawing is labeled telegraphy and is signed by two witnesses. His attorney (name undeciphered) signed A. Graham Bell's name as inventor.

Suggested Teaching Activities for Document #9

A. Setting the stage
  1. Read aloud: Quackenbush, Robert M. *Ahoy! Ahoy! Are You There? A Story of Alexander Graham Bell.* Prentice-Hall, 1981. A humorous account of events in the life of the inventor of the telephone.
  2. Read aloud: Parker, Steve. *Alexander Graham Bell and the Telephone.* Chelsea, 1995. An fact-filled account of Bell's development of the telephone.
  3. Suggest that students locate at least one fact about inventor Alexander Graham Bell. This might be an opportunity to utilize keyword searches in both the library media catalog and on CD-ROM encyclopedia discs.
B. Introduction and discussion
  1. Display a transparency of the schematic diagram of the patent application. Discuss the drawing.
     a. What do you think this drawing shows?
     b. Is there anything familiar on this document?

     c. What is the date of the document?

     d. Do you recognize any of the names on this document?

     e. What do you know about these people or the drawing itself?

     f. What questions do you have because of this drawing?

2. Provide a few dates and verify that the information fits with this document. Dates such as Bell's age (if he were only 12 in 1876 it might be questionable that this document was indeed the same Alexander Graham Bell.)

C. Activity suggestions

1. Discuss the purposes and procedures for procuring a patent. Why would anyone want a patent? The authority for the government's role in granting patents can be found in the Constitution.

2. Investigate Alexander Graham Bell and his other inventions and accomplishments.

3. Investigate the role a man named Watson had in the invention process.

4. Discuss other inventions that relied on electricity. Set up a model of an electrical circuit.

5. Research other inventions that were granted patents in the 1870s.

6. List other inventions that Bell worked on developing.

Document #9

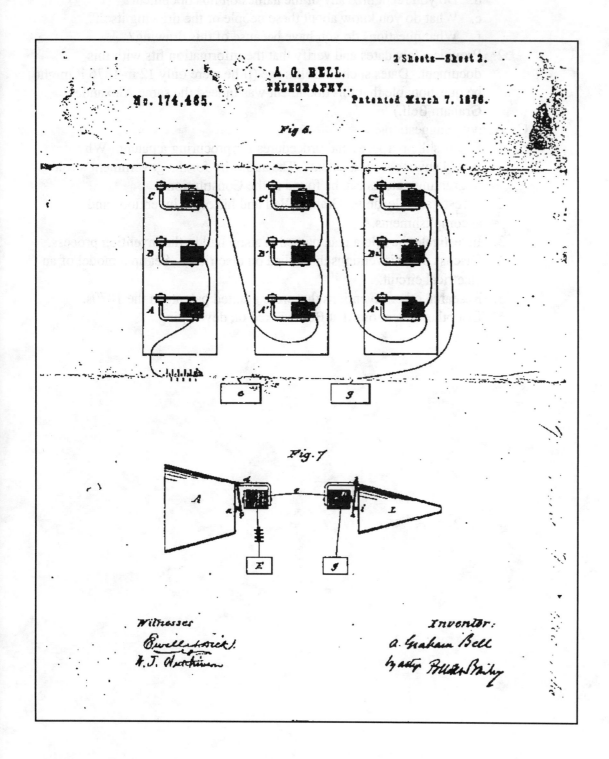

Chapter 4
Moving to a Larger Research Project

Adults seldom write information-only reports as students are often asked to write. In contrast, reports generated in the adult world often use information to support a position or a decision to impact future individual or company actions. The information included in the report is carefully selected to meet the task defined or to answer a question. Some use business reports to justify assigning report writing in school. The fact that school and business reports differ in their purpose and development is often overlooked.

Sometimes student researchers are asked to create a report in a non-written form. This type of reporting varies little from the written report. The researcher learns about a subject and constructs a product to demonstrate that information. The product is often incidental to the research so long as it ties in some way to the topic. Even a multimedia production is used basically to share what has been learned about a topic. One class spent weeks learning about the Native Americans who populated the plains of the United States. They were scheduled to teach another school class about the Plains Indians. The instructor group arrived with each child's face painted with war paint thinking that painting their faces made them Indians. They had missed understanding why and how Native Americans painted their faces.

A defined and authentic task gives research a focus so the researcher will recognize when she or he has found enough appropriate information. Without a goal, whether or not one has enough information is a judgment call by the researcher or by someone directing the research. Information becomes a function of quantity not quality instead of responding to need. If a goal is stated, the research is complete when information answers the question, assists in making the decision, or completes the task identified.

Authentic research often develops in conjunction with hands-on learning activities of many classrooms today. Hands-on learning activities are effective and essential. Experiments allow students to learn firsthand about science through primary research. Math concepts can be used to build scale models. Those learning about business and careers can participate in job-shadowing or activities that give the student firsthand knowledge. These are ready-made opportunities for primary research. Historical topics can be pursued through interviewing those who lived in the era or examining primary documents from the period. Primary research activities allow students to move from copying the opinions of others to constructing their own meanings and drawing their own conclusions.

Breaking Out of the Copy and Report Mold

Some educational literature speaks of using inquiries as an alternative to reports. Despite the basic rhetoric the major differences seen in most classrooms are that report topics are teacher assigned (or assigned within a list of choices) and reported in written form, while inquiry topics are chosen by the student or group of students with teacher guidance and findings in an inquiry are often reported with models, dramatic productions, art representations or videos.

Inquiry products should result naturally from the research information. In actual practice, students researching Native American Indians, for example, build paper and stick teepee (tipi) that bear little resemblance to the actual abode in either scale or materials. The object constructed often shows little about the real lifestyle of the Plains Indians but demonstrates that learning has been superficial. If there is a mention of a "rain dance," students might include that in their demonstration of learning—with little real information about the tradition and sacredness of the dance. The previous war paint is another example of using catch-all information with little thought to the real purpose of presenting it. The fact that the students videotaped the dance and showed it as a multimedia presentation seemed to be justification enough. If the only difference in an inquiry is a product other than a written report then the distinction is not significant. It is still a report of information (or misinformation) gleaned from secondary sources.

Using the inquiry method can provide immense opportunities for hands-on research, meaningful products, and building critical thinking skills. To move the inquiry beyond the mere crafts approach to a meaningful demonstration of learning, the research perspective must change. Researchers sent out to "find all the information you can" with no goal in sight are handicapped. First, how will the students know when they have found enough information? Second, how will they know what information they need to find? Third, why do the researchers want to learn about this topic?

Authentic investigations result from a need to know in order to produce a product or to answer a question. The investigations result in an action or a product—and investigators know goals before they begin. For example, I may investigate window shades and blinds. The investigation is geared toward the need to determine what type of shades or blinds I wish to purchase for my dining room windows. I do not want to find out all there is to know about shades and blinds; I need enough information to allow me to make a decision. In real life, I cannot imagine wanting to learn everything about shades and blinds unless I were designing my own. Information regarding ease of use, cleaning, and durability, will allow me to demonstrate my learning. It would be unrealistic to say to oneself—"Now, let's see what I could do to show my family that I know all about shades and blinds." That doesn't happen. Now, transfer the idea to the research we ask of student learners. The amount and depth of information needed will be determined by the task or goal.

Some educators have devised innovative ways for students to report information they have gathered. For example, a class studying states was asked to identify a state, gather as much information as they could and to use that information and a thesaurus to construct an alliterative paragraph about the state. "The ice cream treat, Eskimo Pies, was developed in a town near Indianola, Iowa. In the 1980s the Midwestern Ice Cream Company was established in Iowa City, Iowa. It became a major industry. Other industries in the state of Iowa include the Maytag Appliance Factory, the Amana Industries (refrigerators, microwaves and other innovative inventions), and the Parker Pen Company whose inking writing instruments have inspired...." A novel way to report information provides some variation on the theme but it really does not get far from "finding out all you can so you can create something that really does not mean anything anyway."A real product that young researchers could create might be a summer travel guide for their families. A class studying the states, for example, might research sites that their families might visit during summer vacation. The title of the brochure could indicate the scope of the research, "Places to Visit on Route 80," "Meandering through the Midwest," or "State-by-State Historical Sites." Individuals or groups might contribute to a collective publication researched, published, and distributed to families who might use it to plan actual trips or make stops along the way to visit relatives or friends. The end product might serve a useful purpose.

Process vs. Product

The debate over which is more important—process or product—will likely continue. The process of research can be applied to different topics, and provides students with the means to be lifelong learners. However, process becomes meaningless without a goal. The goal turns the research process into a problem-solving situation, a research project with a purpose.

The goal must reflect desire to create the product or complete a task. I once walked into a middle school and saw 90 mobiles, hanging from the ceiling, each featuring Canada and its provinces. The teacher displayed them as a demonstration that her students were "actively involved" in learning. I found it amazing that 90 students wanted to make mobiles to show how much they had learned. Do you suppose that one of them wanted to plan a trip to Canada for a family vacation? Perhaps one had a parent who enjoyed fishing and she or he might have wanted to learn the great fishing spots in the Canadian wilderness or the type of fish common to Canada. Perhaps a future zookeeper found it interesting to locate the zoos in Canada and investigating how their zoo operations compared with those in the United States. Others might have wanted to learn about Canadian colleges, or the medical system, or the government. In fact, almost every mobile featured the provinces of Canada, the Canadian flag, and similar representations.

Setting the goal for research goes beyond "everything we can find out." Many school districts have prescribed curriculum topics so the first step is to introduce the general topic, and to learn enough about it to ascertain what specific students might want to learn. Recently some fourth- and fifth-grade students were given the opportunity to create a Web site focusing on literacy and the state of Iowa. It was Iowa's sesquicentennial and the state's literacy council and the Iowa Reading Association were interested in working with students to focus the world on literacy and the opportunities in Iowa.

For the Web site students generated topics, researched information, wrote the copy, and designed the pages. They worked with a Web designer to compose and construct the pages. Their research took them to public libraries, to a bookstore established in 1893, through old newspapers, into historic books, and to visit with people with stories to tell. They read, conducted telephone interviews, wrote letters, and gathered information. Their final product showcased and let the world share their findings. They learned about secondary sources, primary sources, and about sifting information to determine what is needed.

One group set out to learn about the oldest bookstore in Iowa. In secondary sources they found that one of the earliest bookstores was established at a private Iowa college in 1887; however, in their own Iowa community they located a wholesale book company that had been established in 1883. Since that bookstore had not been listed in the secondary sources they concluded that perhaps other bookstores in Iowa were established even earlier. Considering the available resources the students concluded that learning about the local bookstore was a prudent move. Since they could not be absolutely certain that it was the first, they reworded the information to read "One of the earliest bookstores in Iowa, if not the earliest, was the O.G Waffle Book Company in Marion, Iowa." The O.G. Waffle Bookhouse was steeped in history and students interviewed the present owner to learn about that history. Much of this information would have been lost to future generations had it not been preserved by the students. They felt good about their discovery and knew that they had satisfied their goal. General statistics about bookstores helped provide a perspective for the information about the historic bookstore. The result of their research now resides on the World Wide Web (URL: http://www.aea10.k12.ia.us/literacy/) and was published in a hard copy of the Web site distributed by the Iowa Reading Association and other cosponsors.

Before students can intelligently decide on a goal they must know enough about a topic to set a task for further learning. When the task is defined they can brainstorm to obtain predictions or ideas on how to gather the information. When possible sources are identified the process of information gathering begins. As the information is found appropriate, facts are recorded and, when enough information is available, is restructured to fulfill requirements of the defined task. The resulting product allows the information to be showcased. Showcasing is simply a means of sharing the product with an audience. In a classroom setting, showcasing often involves an opportunity for students to ask how the information was obtained and what other interesting incidental learning the researcher found on the way toward the goal. Showcasing in this age of multimedia productions can take the form of a computerized media production on videotape, a CD-ROM disc, or a Web site on the Internet.

Organizing the Research Process

Beginning research without a plan is like setting out to visit a friend in another state without knowing where the friend lives or having identified the highways to get there. Organizing the research can help students know where they are going and what they need to do. Many structures for research are being promoted. One of the more popular is the Big Six Skills developed and popularized by Michael B. Eisenberg and Robert E. Berkowitz and is detailed in their book, *Information Problem-Solving: The Big Six Skills Approach to Library & Information Skills Instruction* (Ablex Publishing Company, 1990). Other structures can be found in *Brainstorms and Blueprints: Teaching Library Research as a Thinking Process* by Barbara K. Stripling and Judy M. Pitts (Libraries Unlimited, 1988) and *Teaching the Library Research Process: A Step-by-Step Program for Secondary School Students* by Carol Collier Kuhlthau (Scarecrow, 1994). While these structures are well thought out and useful, they are geared to the secondary school student and seem to have little emphasis on primary research and primary documents.

A Structure for Researchers

The S.P.I.R.R.E. structure presented here combines the best components of many information-gathering structures and works for elementary school students. It has been developed through restructuring the approaches in the materials cited above. Whether teachers choose S.P.I.R.R.E. or a structure developed by Eisenberg, Berkowitz, Stripling, Pitts, Kuhlthau, or another researcher, the important component to information gathering is that a task be defined early in the process and a systematic approach be followed.

The S.P.I.R.R.E. (pronounced spire) structure represents a six-step process. The acronym will assist students in following procedural steps toward an organized information search.

S.P.I.R.R.E. Research

Select and define a task

Predict strategies for information gathering

Information gathering

Record selected information

Restructure the information for the task

Evaluate and showcase

S.P.I.R.R.E. research structure accommodates the usual secondary resources but can include primary documents and resources. While print materials are important secondary resources, S.P.I.R.R.E. emphasizes using primary resources and technological connections whenever appropriate. For example: many think of the Internet for accessing information. Web searches take an immense amount of time even with a powerful search engine. Although while much information can be up-to-date the fact of its being on the Internet does not guarantee that the information is more up-to-date than print sources. Internet information must be assessed for recency and credibility in the same manner as print sources. CD-ROMs offer access to information in a novel and interesting form. Students can see and hear experts and experience their research process. One example is Scholastic's *Smart Book* series of CD-ROMs, for example, *Exploring the Titanic*[1] (Scholastic, 1994). Listed by the publisher as appropriate for grades 3-8, this CD-ROM tells the story of Ballard's 1986 exploration of the gigantic ship that sank in the Atlantic Ocean 74 years earlier. Not only does the disc read the book but it provides a time line of the *Titanic* and world events and it makes users privy to reactions of people to the news, provides background information and shares facts about the luxurious ship that was thought to be unsinkable. In one segment of the disc, users watch a movie of Robert Ballard talking about discovering the *Titanic*. In another segment, users can read a letter written by Emma Schabert while she was on board the rescue ship, *Carpathia*. Relatives of those who died in the sinking react to the exploration, and graphic presentations show some artifacts that were brought up from the sunken ship as well as a depiction of the sinking itself. This electronic book provides users with primary resources to which most would not ever have access. Graphics recreate hundreds of rooms, gymnasium, swimming pool, and several restaurants for users to tour. Eyewitnesses and several of the 700 survivors share their memories. Students researching topics on explorers, disasters, treasures beneath the sea, or historical events might find this type of CD-ROM a valuable part of their research. Some material is secondary resource information but copies of the documents from the survivors and the firsthand interviews are examples of primary resources.

The S.P.I.R.R.E. research structure allows student researchers to use primary research, such as interviews and documents, and all types of secondary materials in their investigation of the task they have defined.

Distinguishing Between Secondary and Primary Research

The structure of a S.P.I.R.R.E. research project incorporates distinguishing secondary from primary research and documents and defining six basic steps of research. Secondary documents are derived from someone else's research. Research obtained by examining secondary documents is secondary research because information has already been synthesized and structured by someone else into a format for sharing. Primary documents are created at the time of the event, for example, birth certificates, driver's licenses, diaries, letters, and entries in family Bibles. Primary research might involve examining primary documents, synthesizing and restructuring the information to meet the defined goal, and determining conclusions or creating a product to meet the goal.

Primary research will include conducting original research to find information not available from others. For example, a class might conduct an inquiry on effectiveness of some standard waste reduction. Students might observe, collect, and measure the waste thrown away at their school in a day. After sponsoring some educational presentations and instituting recycling and waste reduction procedures in their school they may make new observations, collections, and measurements. Comparing the results of those measurements with the earlier study should yield information that allows students to make their own determinations and interpretations regarding the effectiveness of waste reduction and recycling efforts. Theirs is primary research. If the students had read and reported statistics about the effectiveness, the research would have been secondary.

The following lessons on primary and secondary research models will help students to identify the types of research and construct meaningful strategies for locating appropriate information to perform their identified tasks.

Lesson 1: Introducing Secondary Sources and Research

Objective:
Researchers will view or read a secondary source about an animal or event in order to develop understanding and a definition of secondary sources.

Materials needed:
A film about an animal or an event or a nonfiction book about the topic, for example, one of the many animal titles by Caroline Arnold.

Introduction:
Introduce the concept of secondary sources by explaining that someone else has gathered and restructured that information into a product to share with a second person. Because students are learning the information from someone else who observed or researched it, the information is secondary. Tell students, "Today we will view (or read) a film (book) about (name the topic) in order to make a list of ten things we know about it."

Procedure:
• View the video or read the book.

• Immediately after the viewing or reading, list at least ten things the group knows about the topic.

• Discuss how students think the producer or author got the information in the video or the book.

• Create a working definition of secondary research and resources.

Key point: Secondary documents provide information that the original researcher felt was important. Accuracy of the information in secondary sources depends on the accuracy of the person reporting it.

Discussion Notes—Accuracy of Secondary Sources

A few years ago I was researching information on Steven Kellogg, a well-known children's book author and illustrator. I had interviewed him several times and had much of the information I needed. I decided to put a poster page in the book I was writing that would provide basic information about the authors profiled. I needed Kellogg's birthdate and decided it was more expedient to check standard biographical sources rather than to contact him by phone or letter. Three sources agreed that Kellogg was born in Norwalk, Connecticut, on October 6, 1941. Because the biographical sources were respected sources, I felt comfortable using the October 6 date and did not question its accuracy. A few years later I was creating a calendar that would feature children's authors and would list birthdays for well-known children's writers and illustrators. Kellogg was the featured author for October. Since the publication of the reference book that profiled Kellogg, I had come across another reference listing October 26 as Kellogg's birthdate. I decided to go to the primary source and telephone Kellogg's household. I learned that Steven Kellogg's actual birthday is October 26, 1941. One researcher had made an error and several other resources followed suit. Kellogg receives birthday cards from fans throughout the month of October—from the 6th to the 26th. I corrected the author calendar but the original book has not been revised and the error remains. The error's presence in the book may extend itself to other references and products that use that source.

Brainstorm other ways that secondary sources might include inaccurate information, for example:

typographic errors
reliance on misquoted or misinterpreted information
interview presented from a person who did not know about the topic
inaccurate recording by the person relaying information

Lesson 2: Introducing Primary Sources

Objective: Researchers will examine primary documents to become acquainted with the concept and use of them.

Materials needed: Photocopies of a sample primary document (letter, election poster, or any available document); transparency made from copy display.

Introduction: Introduce the concept of primary documents. Examples are birth certificates, letters, speeches, census records, photographs, diaries, and historical documents.

Procedure: Examine selected primary documents (select new ones related to local or school history, or a personal document, or use one or more of the documents used in earlier exercises) and discuss information a researcher might glean from them.

Key point: Documents created at the time of an event provide information that can lead an observant researcher to formulate conclusions about the person.

Lesson 3: Introducing Primary Research

Objective:	Researchers will gather information by engaging in primary research in order to understand the nature of primary sources.
Materials needed:	Chart or transparency of suggested research questions. See suggestions under Procedure. (Note: In preparing the chart do not include suggested methods listed in parentheses. Students will generate ideas for collecting data.)
Introduction:	Introduce data gathering with a question such as, "How many times during an hour, do children at _____ school sharpen their pencils?" Discuss how data could be gathered and recorded. Then tell students that today they will become primary researchers.
Procedure:	• Display the list of suggested research questions and select and identify a question to pursue. Similar questions might be substituted using any that keeps the research activity compact.

☐ What is the first thing students do upon entering the library media center? (Observe and collect data.)

☐ Of the students who attend _____school, what time in the morning do most get up? (Survey students and tally the data.)

☐ What is the most popular television show of fourth- and fifth-grade students? (Interview a select sampling of fourth and fifth graders; collect the data.)

      □ How many students are absent on (specify day)?
(Survey each classroom teacher or interview the
attendance clerk at the school.)

      □ How many students in your classroom get a drink
of water during a 30-minute period of time?
(Observe and record data.)

- Brainstorm methods for gathering the appropriate
data. Be sure the methods will result in firsthand
observation or data gathering rather than relying on
observations and interpretations of others.

- Use the collected data to formulate conclusions and
theories.

      Key point: Observing and collecting firsthand knowledge about a topic
or person is the core activity of primary research. Observations, interviews,
and surveys are three techniques for obtaining firsthand information.

S.P.I.R.R.E.

      Before beginning the extended research project, the general structure of
the project should be shared and discussed. The following lesson will focus on
sharing that structure and exploring the steps or questions in lessons following
introduction to the structure.

Lesson 4: Introducing the S.P.I.R.R.E. Research and Problem Solving Structure

Objectives:	Students will identify the steps of the S.P.I.R.R.E. Research and Problem Solving Structure.
Materials needed:	Chart or transparency listing steps in the S.P.I.R.R.E. Research and Problem Solving Structure. (See Appendix A.) Research binder (a notebook to organize research materials in this and following lessons).
Anticipatory set:	Using a chart or transparency, show students the acronym S.P.I.R.R.E. and tell them that this acronym represents a structure to help organize research activities. You may have to explain what that word means.
Introduction:	Show the complete chart representing S.P.I.R.R.E. and explain that each letter of the acronym stands for a step of research and problem-solving activities.

Procedure: Using the S.P.I.R.R.E. chart, ask students to share what they think might be involved in each step of the structure. Guide students to the definitions below.

S.P.I.R.R.E. Research

1. **Select and identify a task.**
   Determine the problem or question and identify informational aspects of the problem. List questions that need to be answered. Decide what information is necessary for solving the problem.

2. **Predict strategies for information gathering.**
   Create a list of possible sources (books, people, libraries, Internet, CD-ROM—be as specific as possible) that might yield the needed information. Brainstorming options for locating information will help determine appropriate strategies.

3. **Information gathering.**
   Students must attempt to use the predicted strategies to acquire information and meet the identified task. This step involves acquiring and using skills to physically locate the resources, the appropriate information, or in the case of interviews, questions that will lead to the needed information.

4. **Record selected information.**
   Once students locate sources and access the information, they must interact with it, for example, read, view, or listen, and decide what is valuable and appropriate to the task. That information must be recorded by making notes or photocopying it so that the student can refer to it during restructuring.

5. **Restructure the information for the task.**
   Applying the information to accomplish the task encompasses restructuring or repackaging it into a format to meet the defined task requirements and synthesizing the information to create a product that will satisfy the goal or defined task.

6. **Evaluate and showcase.**
   Students must evaluate the problem-solving process and showcase the results; they should assess how effectively and efficiently they accomplished the task.

Culmination: Review steps of S.P.I.R.R.E. research structure and tell students that the next research session will utilize the structure to begin a research project.

Key point: Getting organized will assist the researcher to focus on activities that will lead to a productive search.

Select and Identify a Task

This stage of the research project is the most crucial. We will determine the problem or question and identify its information aspects. Subsequent lessons will list the questions that need to be answered and decide what type of information is necessary for solving the problem.

The lesson plan assumes researchers will have some latitude in selecting the topic and the product for which they will be responsible. Before beginning this phase the teacher must decide whether to allow total self-selection or exert some degree of control. Considerations influencing the decision include resource and energy limitations, the research sophistication expected, and whether or not a major objective is to extend concepts to the established curriculum. Themes, community extensions—people or places, and issues discussed in class will all affect the necessary degree of control. Once these decisions have been made, the teacher can select and define the research task.

Lesson 5: Finding an Interest (Topic)

Objective:

Each researcher will identify topics which interest her or him.

Materials needed:

- Copy of *Topics That May Interest Me* graphic organizer for each student. (See Appendix A.)

- Copy of *Choosing a Topic* graphic organizer for each student. (See Appendix A.)

Introduction:

Peruse the nonfiction area of the library media center to stimulate interest in specific topics that might be the subject of student research. Ask students to use the *Topics That May Interest Me* organizer to list any they find.

Procedure:

1. Utilize the interest charts to instigate a discussion of topics that individuals in the research group have identified.

2. Identify new topics that might be the subject of research.

3. Engage in *research talk*—discuss what topics might be interesting for further research. Collaborate and share already-known ideas about the topics and things students might want to know about each.

4. Each student or research group should use the graphic organizer *Choosing a Topic* to list at least five.

Culmination:

After the *Choosing a Topic* organizer has been completed culminate the lesson by asking students to spend time, before the next research discussion, considering their most interesting topic. During the next lesson students will utilize the *Choosing a Topic* organizer to identify questions and a specific topic and task.

Key point: A research topic must be accompanied by questions about it. Identifying a topic alone is not enough. Researchers must also know what type of information they would like to know and what they would like to do with it.

Lesson 6: Examining My Options

Objective:

Each researcher or research group will narrow its topic of interest to one major topic.
Each researcher or research group will identify and select a specific task to be accomplished through the proposed research.

Materials needed:

• Copies of *Choosing a Topic* from previous lesson.

• Transparency, copies or a large chart of *Action Words*: *Identifying a Task*. (See Appendix A.)

Introduction:

Display a copy of a completed *Choosing a Topic* organizer. Use it as a model to talk through the process of completing the chart and narrowing options.

Procedure:

1. Make a composite list of all the research topics the research group members have identified.

2. As a group, discuss the topics, questions and ideas for research projects that others have.

3. Engage in group research talk—collaborate and share ideas about appropriate refinements to the questions.

4. Discuss possibilities relating to specific topics and encourage students to generate other possibilities.

5. A conference with each individual or research group will help them to examine their options for specific research topics.

6. During the teacher-researcher conference use the *Action Words: Identifying a Task* chart to help refine the information being sought. The conferences may take a day or two to meet with all students, but should help finalize the task or question and its wording. For example: If students wish to research their city, specific questions might include: For whom is our city named? When did it become a city? What early events were important in our city's history? During the conference, these questions might be translated into tasks to allow sharing of the information. The question "For whom is our city named?" might result in a campaign to build a memorial to the city founder. The question will help narrow the topic but the decision on sharing will structure the type of research needed. A biography of the founder will require searching historical documents and synthesizing information into a presentation, whereas the campaign to build a memorial to the city founder will involve learning enough about the person to sell the idea to a focus group who might assist the project, designing that memorial project, and then obtaining support to implement the plan. The memorial might be as elaborate as a statue in the town park, a memorial article in the city's newspaper, a day-long celebration, or a mayor's declaration naming a specific day in the founder's honor. Each project will require a slightly different focus in the research.

7. Students should record their selected tasks in their research binders. The actual format for presentation need not be finalized yet. A biography, for example, might be formatted as a book, a video, a page on the city's Internet Web site, or a play. An historical brochure might be a printed brochure or might be a video featuring historic sites.

Culmination: Each researcher will have a specific task identified and written in specific terms. After the selected task has been recorded ask students to think about the information they will need to complete the task.

Key point: Once the topic is selected a specific task must be identified in relation to that topic. The task will influence the research to be undertaken.

Predicting Strategies, Information Gathering and Recording

During these steps of the research structure researchers should assess their task to predict where they might locate information to answer questions or make decisions connected with their selected task. Once researchers have prepared a list of potential information sources they should proceed to the information gathering stage.

Lesson 7: The Research—Predicting, Information Gathering, and Recording

Objective:	Each researcher or research group will predict and identify potential resources.
	Each researcher or research group will gather resources.
	Each researcher or research group will select and record appropriate information.
Materials needed:	• Chart paper and magic marker or blank transparency and transparency marker.
	• Copies of the *Getting Organized—Where Can I Get Information?: Secondary Sources* and *Getting Organized—Where Can I Get Information?: Primary Research Activities and Primary Sources* for each student. (See Appendix A for each graphic organizer.)
Introduction:	Tell researchers that they will brainstorm a list of resources that they might use to find information.
Procedure:	1. As a group, use chart paper or the transparency to record resource suggestions locating information. As the suggestions are recorded use different color markers to indicate secondary or primary resources, or primary research opportunities. Alternatively, draw three columns and put suggestions into the appropriate column. Guide researchers to identify at least the following resources:
	a. Secondary sources: books, periodical articles, videos; references such as encyclopedias, CD-ROMs, Internet sources, special reference books.
	b. Primary research: locations for observation,

events for participation or observation, surveys to conduct, people to interview.

   c. Primary documents: documents relating to the topic, such as letters, diaries, photographs.

2. Pass out copies of the two *Getting Organized...*graphic organizers and ask researchers to use them to list potential sources before they begin their in-depth research.

3. To fill out the *Getting Organized...*charts, students will need to check the library media center catalog, browse reference shelves, think about organizations and people in your community, and brainstorm possible sources of information.

4. As each possible source is identified it should be recorded on the *Getting Organized...*charts. The charts will suggest specific paths for the research. As resources are explored, new resource possibilities may be added to the *Getting Organized...*charts.

5. After completing the charts, researchers should begin the actual research and record appropriate information in their research binder. These activities will span several blocks of time and will require teacher facilitation.

6. Remind researchers that they are on a quest for information to help them complete their selected task, not on a quest for all the information they can find on the topic.

7. Mini-lessons focusing on types of reference materials should be used with individuals or small groups as the need arises and in the context of their research. For example, a task such as constructing a scale drawing of a colonial kitchen will require information about colonial kitchens and utensils. Once the researchers have located a resource on colonial living, they will need to be able to use the index to find the specific pages on colonial kitchens or utensils. If they do not know about using an index, a mini-lesson may be utilized. Optional library skills mini-lessons might include:

   a. Using an index.

   b. Determining the scope of a reference source.

   c. Determining the relevancy of a specific source.

d. Using the table of contents to locate information in a book.

e. Checking the copyright date to ascertain recency.

f. Learning about the author or the resource person to determine credibility.

g. Using the library media center catalog: author, subject, title and Boolean searches.

h. Accessing the Internet or online services to locate information—using URL (addresses); search engines; bookmarks.

i. Using a CD-ROM to locate information.

j. Accessing area libraries from a remote source (activating a modem access). You may wish to use the *Mini-lesson Record Sheet—Library Skills* to keep track of which students have been involved in specific instruction groups. (See Appendix A.)

8. Students interested in interviewing a source of information should be introduced to the interviewing organizers. (See Lesson 9.)

Culmination: When the research is completed each researcher or research group will have a folder of notes, copies, and other recorded information. In Lesson 12, researchers will evaluate their information and, depending on the evaluation, proceed to one of the final steps.

Key point: Information gathering is a time-consuming process requiring students to think about possibilities beyond the initial resource. Having a specific task permits recording only relevant information.

Lesson 8: Creating a Time Line for the Research Project

Objective: Each researcher or research group will develop a time line for their research project.
Each researcher or research group will determine what activities need to be accomplished to meet the objective of the identified task.

Materials needed: Local phone book.
Note cards (optional).
Copies of *Schedule Calendar.* (See Appendix A.)
Copies of *Project/Research Planning Guide.* (See Appendix A.)

Introduction: Discuss the class schedule for completion of the research project. Provide copies of the planning calendar and of the daily planner for each student's use.

Procedure:

1. As a group, reach a consensus for a completion date. (This date might need to be adjusted as the group gets further into the research. However, it is important that a time line be established so that discussion regarding the actual project will include amount of time available.)

2. As a class, determine some bench marks or basic target dates for completing phases of the research. Refer to the S.P.I.R.R.E. structure. Don't forget that the first evaluation may result in revisiting the information and recording phases of the research. Allow for some regrouping in terms of identified task and additional information gathering.

3. Each researcher should develop a tentative calendar or schedule for research activities and place it in the research binder.

4. The *Project/Research Planning Guide* should be used to map out detailed daily activities the first week of research. Each week a new weekly planner should be filled out. As the teacher you may ask students to schedule specific times to attend mini-lessons or you may schedule groups into the library media center for research. Ideally, the library media specialist will be available to work with small groups throughout the week. This is preferable to scheduling an entire class into the library media center at one time. Organization and collaboration between the classroom teacher and the library media specialist may result in one group having a mini-lesson with the classroom teacher and another group researching in the library media center, while the other groups are taking notes from resources obtained earlier or making arrangements and preparing for interviews and on-site visits.

Culmination:

Post an enlargement of the general calendar in the room or have it available on a transparency in order to refer to the schedule daily.

Key point: Bench marking specific activities on a schedule or calendar will assist in keeping researchers accountable for their progress.

Lesson 9: The Interview
(A mini-lesson for those who have scheduled a personal interview)

Objective:	Each researcher who has scheduled an interview will become acquainted with general question-writing techniques.
	Each researcher will generate appropriate questions for the interview.
	Each researcher will prepare for the interview, make the contact, and record the time and place of the interview.
	Each researcher will conduct scheduled interview.
Materials needed:	• Copy of *Getting Ready for the Interview: Helpful Ideas for Writing Questions* for each student. (See Appendix A.) • Copy of *Getting Ready for the Interview* for each student. (See Appendix A.)
Introduction:	Mention that each of them has identified a person they would like to interview to learn more about their topic. Tell students that today's discussion will help them prepare for the interviews.
Procedure:	1. Once students know whom they would like to interview and when they can meet with the person to be interviewed the students should contact that person to arrange an appointment. Students should record the time and date on their *Getting Ready for the Interview* sheet.
	2. Students who have scheduled interviews should work through the *Getting Ready for the Interview: ...Writing Questions* list of helpful ideas. Students should brainstorm their own lists of categories and words about their topic or task but may collaborate with other group members. The categories and words can help researchers formulate questions.
	3. Read together the considerations for writing questions and discuss the implications of each.
	4. Students should write the questions they think they might want to ask on a separate piece of paper and then hold a mock interview with a fellow classmate.

Interview etiquette should be discussed including introducing oneself, being a listener, and thanking the interviewed person.

5. Proposed questions should be reviewed to decide if an expert answer is needed. Can the question be answered through secondary research? Keep in mind that an interview should be used to ascertain information not available from traditional sources, or to verify information from those sources.

6. Questions should be revised based on results of the mock interview and the question review above. The final version of the questions should be recorded on the *Getting Ready for the Interview* sheet.

7. For convenience and easier supervision, it is helpful if interviews are held at the school site or by phone. Sometimes it is important to view a person's work site. In those cases, the teacher should arrange for someone to accompany the student and make a special effort to see that all precautions are taken to make the interview a positive and meaningful experience.

8. Meet the person and conduct the interview. Students should:
   a. Be aware that follow-up questions may result from the original questions planned.
   b. Confirm the correct spelling of the person's name and his or her address (so that a thank-you message can be written after the interview, even though the student will thank the person).
   c. Often student interviewers have a difficult time listening and writing notes from the information being provided. Students might consider asking if the interview may be audiotaped so that notes can be accurately recorded.

Culmination: Information gathered in an interview will need to be sifted for relevant material and a summary of the interview must be written.

Key point: Preparation will help make the interview a positive information-gathering activity that yields much information.

Lesson 10: Taking Notes

Objective:	Each researcher will record information sources and will take appropriate notes from them whether the sources are primary, secondary, or data from primary research.
Materials needed:	Transparencies of *Recording Information: Taking Notes.* (See Appendix A.)
Introduction:	A first step in information gathering is to locate necessary background information about the topic in order to build on that information with primary research or sources. Students should develop a means for keeping track of information and its location in order to double-check conflicting material, and to record the information.
Procedure:	1. Once a source is identified, a source card should be prepared. Share examples of the card indicating the format for recording sources. Note that this information is recorded only for purposes of rechecking or revisiting the original source. If you wish students to prepare a formal bibliography, refer to a style manual and use examples in the selected style manual to format the actual bibliography.

a. The card should list:
   (1) Author (last name first)
   (2) Title
   (3) Illustrator
   (4) Publisher of the book or producer of the nonprint item
   (5) Copyright, interview, or photo date
   (6) Source number in the upper right-hand corner. Use consecutive numbers as sources are located.
   (7) The locations in the lower left-hand corner specify public, school, or other local library, phone, mail, Internet or online service.

2. Note cards should be used to record appropriate information. Students should be encouraged to record only one idea with the source notation on each card.

   After reading the book, accessing the nonprint informational source, or conducting the interview, the student should identify significant facts and record each fact or statement on an individual note card.

a. Note the source number in the upper right-hand corner.

b. Record the fact on the card.

c. If the fact is a direct quote use quotation marks.

d. Indicate the page or other identifying information on the location of the fact. If the fact was gleaned from an article within an encyclopedia, an Internet page, or another such source, indicate the article's title. If the source is an interview, the source number will suffice since the source card will indicate date and time of interview.

Note: If it is decided to put notes on standard sized paper, adapt procedures to accommodate that format. In all circumstances the use of source cards is recommended. Students may use a single page for notes from each information source so that the source number can be recorded at the top of each page.

Culmination: Each researcher should practice creating a source card and an information card for a source or a fact from that source.

Key point: Successful researchers have a procedure for recording the information they locate.

Lesson 11: Evaluating Where We Are
(Lessons 11 and 12 are evaluative lessons—Choose either option.)

Objective: Each researcher or research group will assess the information they have at this point.

Each researcher or research group will determine whether the next step is to restructure or to gather more information.

Materials needed: Copy of the list of evaluation questions *Evaluate and Assess—1* (see Appendix A) for each researcher.

Transparency of the list of evaluation questions *Evaluate and Assess—1.* Students may reach this stage at varying times during the research procedure and this lesson may then be adapted to an individual or small group activity.

Introduction: Introduce and discuss the philosophy of evaluating during the process in order to regroup or reassess what has been accomplished thus far. Introduce the list of evaluation questions by using the overhead transparency.

Procedure: 1. Ask researchers to use their copies of the evaluation questions to assess where they are and what the next step should be.

2. Allow time for researchers to self-evaluate their research thus far.
   - Have I located enough information for me to determine the solution to the question or to help me solve the problem?
   - Or can I modify the question or task to fit the available information?
   - Have I learned what I wanted to learn about the topic?
   - Am I ready to share the results of my task or my solution to the question?
   - Are there any additional questions that need to be answered as a result of the information discovered in this research?
   - Do I have any problems with this research that I need to discuss with the teacher?

3. Hold a conference with each student to discuss his or her evaluation.

4. Assist students in reaching a decision as to the next step. Either the information gathered is sufficient to meet the identified task or more information is needed, leaving the researcher with two options:
   a. If there is enough information, the researcher should restructure it, or
   b. If the information is insufficient, the researcher could choose:
      (1) to revisit the information gathering and recording steps and gather additional information in order to meet the task objectives; or
      (2) to redefine the selected task to match the available information. Note that the overall task would not be changed, but might be revised to fit the available information. For example, a task such as locating and visiting the oldest library in the state and presenting a

photo essay about it on an Internet Web site might meet snags if it is difficult to positively identify the oldest library, or the oldest library is identifiable but too far away for the researcher to obtain pictures and no response has been received from written inquiries. In either situation the task might be redefined to focus on "one of the oldest" libraries—one that is close enough to visit and photograph. The task would not be totally changed but would be redefined because of the information and situation. In most cases, if the identified task is redefined, the information gathering steps must still be revisited and completed with the newly identified task in mind.

Culmination:
A decision regarding the next step is made. If researchers need to go back to the gathering stage, a conference should be held to ascertain what additional resources are needed; otherwise, they should move to the restructuring phase of the research activity.

Key point: Assessing the information in terms of the identified task allows the researcher to determine when the process of gathering and recording is sufficient.

Lesson 12: Evaluating Where We Are—An In-Progress Sharing Session

(Lessons 11 and 12 are evaluative lessons—Choose either option.)

Objective:
Each researcher or research group will assess the information they have at this point.
Each researcher will engage in an in-progress sharing session.
Each researcher or research group will determine whether the next step is to restructure or to gather more information.

Materials needed:
Copy of the list of evaluation questions *Evaluate and Assess—1* (see Appendix A) for each researcher.

Transparency of the list of evaluation questions *Evaluate and Assess—1*. Students may reach this stage at varying times during the research procedure and this lesson may then be adapted to an individual or small group activity.

Introduction:

Discuss the philosophy of evaluating during the process in order to regroup or reassess what has been accomplished thus far. Suggest that information sometimes can be clarified if that information is shared in a preliminary session. Introduce the list of evaluation questions that might be used to guide the discussion by using the overhead transparency.

Procedure:

1. Ask researchers to use their copies of the evaluation questions to assess where they are and what the next step should be.
2. Allow time for researchers to self-evaluate their research thus far and to select and identify the information they might wish to share with a partner.
3. Each researcher should select a partner and a time to discuss the selected task and the information they wish to share. Together they should discuss the evaluation of the progress made so far.
   - Have I located enough information for me to determine the solution to the question or to help me solve the problem?
   - Or can I modify the question or task to fit the available information?
   - Have I learned what I wanted to learn about the topic?
   - Am I ready to share the results of my task or my solution to the question?
   - Are there any additional questions that now need to be answered as a result of the information discovered in this research?
   - Do I have any problems with this research that I need to discuss with the teacher?
4. In consultation with the partner and the teacher the researcher should reach a decision as to the next step. Either the information gathered is sufficient to meet the identified task or more information is needed, leaving the researcher with two options:
   a. If there is enough information, the researcher should restructure it, or
   b. If the information is insufficient, the researcher could choose:
      (1) to revisit the information gathering and recording steps and gather additional information in order to meet the task objectives; or
      (2) to redefine the selected task to match the available information. Note that the overall task would not be changed, but might be

revisited to fit the available information. For example, a task such as locating and visiting the oldest library in the state and presenting a photo essay about it on an Internet Web site might meet snags if it is difficult to positively identify the oldest library, or the oldest library is identifiable but too far away for the researcher to obtain pictures and no response has been received from written inquiries. In either situation the task might be redefined to focus on "one of the oldest" libraries—one that is close enough to visit and photograph. The task would not be totally changed but would be redefined because of the information and situation. In most cases, if the identified task is redefined, the information gathering steps must still be revisited and completed with the newly identified task in mind.

Culmination: A decision regarding the next step is made. If researchers need to go back to the gathering stage, a conference should be held to ascertain what additional resources are needed; otherwise, they should move to the restructuring phase of the research activity.

Key point: Assessing the information in terms of the identified task allows the researcher to determine when the process of gathering and recording is sufficient.

Restructuring the Information

Once the information is gathered and researchers feel that they have sufficient information to answer the questions or to make the decisions associated with the task, they should to select a product that will showcase the information and share it with others.

Lesson 13: Selecting a Product to Showcase the Information

Objective: Each researcher will select a product to meet the objectives of the identified task.

Materials needed: Transparency of chart—*How Shall I Tell Others About What I Know?* or *Choosing What to Do.* (See Appendix A.)

Introduction: Now that the information has been gathered to answer the questions identified as the selected task, students need to restructure the information to either meet the goal directly, or to create a specific product to showcase it.

Procedure:

1. Review the questions or task originally identified as the goal for this research.
2. In some cases a product will have been designated in the initial stages; in other cases only a target product might have been suggested. This is the time to finalize plans for the product that might be showcased. For example, in the beginning stages a student may have wanted to showcase the information as a multimedia production. Now the researcher may refine that product design and decide if the information is more suited to a video or music production, a CD-ROM, or an Internet Web page with graphics. Part of the decision will rest with the equipment capabilities available for student productions. Another consideration is the type of information one obtained and whether the student has permission rights to reproduce pictures and publish quotes.
3. Consult a copyright guide if a student plans to publish a research project in a form accessible to an audience larger than the classroom. For example, students who want to showcase their work on the Internet will need signed permission forms for publishing pictures and quotes of more than 25 words. (See sample permission form in Appendix A.)

Culmination:

Each researcher will list her or his potential product on a chart displayed in the classroom.

Key point: A product will allow researchers to showcase their learning.

Lesson 14: The Restructuring—Producing the Product

During this phase of the research project each student will plan and create a product and prepare to showcase her or his learning. The teacher should assist students in locating appropriate materials and in the production of the product. For example, if the product involves a video recording, procedures should be discussed and a video recording camera be made available to the researcher. Others may need access to an HTML editor for producing a Web site. Students are responsible for tracking their own progress, seeking help with equipment and production, implementing the plan, and developing the product.

Evaluation

The final stage of the research project is sharing the information with others through the product. In the process students will determine whether the information and product satisfy the objective and goals of the research project.

Lesson 15: The Showcase and Evaluation

Select a time and place for the research showcase. Students should set up their projects and products and be available to answer questions. Peers and other guests should be invited to browse the display of projects.

Following the showcase the overall project should be evaluated.

Give researchers copies of the final evaluation checklist (see Appendix A) and ask them to prepare an evaluation of their own products. The evaluation might be filled out independently and discussed or filled out during an evaluation conference with the teacher.

- Did I locate enough information to determine the solution to the question or to help me solve the problem?
- Or was I able to modify the question or task to fit the available information?
- Does my product share with others the results of my task or the solution I have reached regarding the question?
- Did I learn what I wanted to learn about the topic?
- If I were to do this project again, would I do anything differently? If yes, what?
- Does my project show others what I have learned or decided?
- Are there any additional questions that now need to be answered as a result of the information discovered in this project?

Lesson 16: Concluding and Reflecting

Once the research project is developed and showcased, ask students to reflect on the activity by writing in their research binder or learning journal. What did they feel they learned? What would they now do differently? Would they choose another topic? Why or why not? Did they enjoy learning?

As the research facilitators, the classroom teacher and the library media specialist should also record their reflections on the activity in writing. Using these reflections the teacher may hold a debriefing session for those involved in the research to engage in research talk and learn from each other's experiences. To celebrate learning, the teacher may bring milk and cookies to share, sit on a carpet in a circle, and just talk.

---

[1] Scholastic, Inc. 555 Broadway, New York, NY 10012-3999; phone: 1-212-343-6878.

<u>Appendix A</u>

Dewey Decimal Classification System

000-099   **General Works**
(examples: encyclopedias, bibliographies)

100-199   **Philosophy**

200-299   **Religion**
(examples: Bibles, Koran, mythological tales)

300-399   **Social Sciences**
(examples: cultures, folklore)

400-499   **Language**
(examples: dictionaries, word origins, alphabet books)

500-599   **Pure Science**
(examples: physics, solar system)

Dewey Decimal Classification System

600-699 Applied Science
(examples: medicine, space travel)

700-799 Fine Arts and Recreation
(examples: sports, music, games)

800-899 Literature
(examples: poems, plays)

900-999 History and Geography
(examples: collective biographies, materials on countries and states)

Dewey Decimal Classification System

000-099 General Works
(encyclopedias, almanacs, etc.)

100-199 Philosophy
(people's thoughts and their way of thinking)

200-299 Religion
(people's ideas about God)

300-399 Social Sciences
(how people live together)

400-499 Language
(how people talk to each other)

500-599 Pure Science
(nature, the world, and the universe)

Dewey Decimal Classification System

600-699 Applied Science
(ways to use science to help us)

700-799 Fine Arts and Recreation
(painting, music, dancing, sports, and games)

800-899 Literature
(storytelling and poetry)

900-999 History and Geography
(people, places, and important events)

Use this chart to help explain the subclassification system. The number in front of the decimal point indicates the general classification. Each number past the decimal point defines the book further and more specifically.

Chart C

Dewey Decimal Classification System

Class: 700-799
             Fine Arts and Recreation

Subclass: 790, recreation
796   athletics and outdoor sports
796.3   ball games
796.31   ball thrown or hit by hand
796.33   ball driven by foot
796.34   racquet games
796.35   ball driven by a club, mallet, or bat
796.352   golf
796.357   baseball

Making a Research Telephone Call

1. Before dialing the telephone:
   a. fill out the person's name, the phone number, and any other information needed on the telephone log;
   b. have your question or questions written on paper;
   c. have paper and pencil available to take notes.

2. Dial the phone number on your log.

3. When the phone is answered, introduce yourself immediately using your first and last names.

4. Mention the school's name and that you are working on a research project. Briefly describe the project.

5. Ask your questions and take notes.

6. When you have asked your questions, say "thank you" and hang up the telephone.

7. If the telephone call has been lengthy (more than one question), write a thank you note and send it.

Telephone Call Log

Date: _____

Caller: _____

Put your first and last names on this blank along with your classroom number.

Name of person
to be called:_____

Address_____

Telephone Number:_____

Topic of interview:_____

Status:

_____ Interviewed

_____ No answer, need to recall

_____ Left message with _____

_____ Other: _____

Follow-up action: _____

_____

_____

_____

_____

Addressing an Envelope

YOUR NAME   PASTE STAMP
STREET ADDRESS   HERE
CITY STATE ZIP CODE

                              NAME
                              DEPARTMENT
                              BUSINESS
                              STREET ADDRESS
                              CITY STATE ZIP CODE

All letters should be UPPERCASE.

No punctuation.

Two spaces between city, state, and zip code.

Two-letter abbreviation used for the state's name.

Use abbreviation for street, circle, as appropriate. See abbreviation
list.

Address printed by computer or hand printed (no cursive).

Abbreviations
For States, Territories, and the District of Columbia

AL	Alabama	NE	Nebraska
AK	Alaska	NV	Nevada
AS	American Samoa	NH	New Hampshire
AZ	Arizona	NJ	New Jersey
AR	Arkansas	NM	New Mexico
CA	California	NY	New York
CO	Colorado	NC	North Carolina
CT	Connecticut	ND	North Dakota
DE	Delaware	MP	North Mariana Islands
DC	District of Columbia	OH	Ohio
FL	Florida	OK	Oklahoma
GA	Georgia	OR	Oregon
GU	Guam	PA	Pennsylvania
HI	Hawaii	PR	Puerto Rico
ID	Idaho	RI	Rhode Island
IL	Illinois	SC	South Carolina
IN	Indiana	SD	South Dakota
IA	Iowa	TN	Tennessee
KS	Kansas	TX	Texas
KY	Kentucky	TT	Trust Territory
LA	Louisiana	UT	Utah
ME	Maine	VT	Vermont
MD	Maryland	VI	Virgin Islands U.S.
MA	Massachusetts	VA	Virginia
MI	Michigan	WA	Washington
MN	Minnesota	WV	West Virginia
MS	Mississippi	WI	Wisconsin
MO	Missouri	WY	Wyoming
MT	Montana		

 Reproducible from *Research Strategies for Moving Beyond Reporting*, by Sharron L. McElmeel (1997, Linworth Publishing, Inc.)

Abbreviations
For Street Suffixes, Directionals, and Locators

AVE	Avenue		N	North
BLVD	Boulevard		S	South
CT	Court		E	East
CTR	Center		W	West
DR	Drive			
EXPY	Expressway			
HTS	Heights			
HWY	Highway			
IS	Island			
JCT	Junction			
LK	Lake			
LN	Lane			
MTN	Mountain			
PKY	Parkway			
PL	Place			
RD	Road			
STA	Station			
ST	Street			
TPKE	Turnpike			
VLY	Valley			
APT	Apartment			
RM	Room			
STE	Suite			
PLZ	Plaza			

Family Tree

_____ (#1)

Your Name

_____ (#2) _____ (#5)

_____ _____

Your Mother's Name Your Father's Name

| |

Your material grandparents: (#3) Your paternal grandparents: (#6)
_____ _____

_____ _____

Your Grandmother's Name Your Grandmother's Name

_____ (#4) _____ (#7)

_____ _____

Your Grandfather's Name Your Grandfather's Name

Looking for Information
Primary Documents

1. Type of document (check one):

__ Advertisement	__ Congressional Report	__ Census Report
__ Letter	__ Map	__ Memorandum
__ Newspaper	__ Patent document	__ Press release
__ Report	__ Telegram	__ Other _____

2. Format and special features of document:

__ Handwritten	__ Typed	__ Letterhead
__ Notations added	__ "RECEIVED" stamp	__ seals or stamps
__ Other _____		

3. Date(s) of document: _____

4. Author (or creator) of the document: _____

   Position (Title): _____

5. Who did the creator think would read the document? _____

6. Document information:

  A. List two things the author said that you think are important:

    1. _____

    2. _____

  B. List two things that you could learn from the document:

    1. _____

    2. _____

  C. List two things you can figure out about life in the United States based on the document:

    1. _____

    2. _____

  D. What is the most valuable piece of information you can glean from this document?

S.P.I.R.R.E. Research

Select and define a task

Predict strategies for information gathering

Information gathering

Record selected information

Restructure the information for the task

Evaluate and showcase

Topics That May Interest Me

Name: _____

On the lines below list topics that you think you might be interested in learning more about. You may want to browse the nonfiction area of the library media center to help you think about some topics and be sure to talk the idea over with friends.

_____   _____

_____   _____

_____   _____

_____   _____

_____   _____

_____   _____

_____   _____

_____   _____

Look over the topics you have listed on the lines above and circle four to six topics that you are most interested in. Then list your choices below.

_____   _____

_____   _____

_____   _____

Circle the one topic you will select for your research.

Reproducible from *Research Strategies for Moving Beyond Reporting*, by Sharron L. McElmeel (1997, Linworth Publishing, Inc.)

Choosing a Topic

Criteria to Consider

1. Write your topic choices in the "topic alternative" blanks in the chart above.

2. Answer the criteria questions by using a scale of 1 to 5 (1 being low and 5 being high).

3. Total the points for each topic.

4. Consider the point totals and other input you have gotten from your teacher and classmates.

5. State your final topic decision.

6. State at least three reasons you have made this decision.

_____

_____

_____

_____

 Reproducible from *Research Strategies for Moving Beyond Reporting*, by Sharron L. McElmeel (1997, Linworth Publishing, Inc.)

Action Words
Identifying a Task

Analyze — Divide the topic into parts and then tell how each of the parts relates to the topic as a whole. Tell how each of the parts relates to each of the other parts.

Assess — Evaluate or give a rating.

Compare — Identify the differences and the similarities between two or more things. Tell about the similarities and the differences.

Contrast — Identify the differences between two or more things and tell about those differences.

Define — Explain the meaning of the word or phrase. If possible, give an example that will help us understand the meaning.

Describe — Give information that will help others recognize this object, person, thing, or idea.

Discuss — Determine what information will help others know about the topic and give that information. Discuss is similar to describe.

Evaluate — Figure out the positive points and negative points about the topic or idea being evaluated. Use those points to help establish your opinion about the topic or idea.

Explain — Provide the details about the topic. The details often will be sequential and provide reasons or causes for something.

Illustrate — Cite specific examples to help others understand your idea or thought.

Relate — Identify and explain how two things are connected or tied together by a common element.

Summarize — Using as few words as possible, provide a brief presentation of the information you have gathered.

Topic: _____

Getting Organized—Where Can I Get Information?
Secondary Sources

Books (Check library media center catalog and other libraries.)

_____

_____

_____

_____

_____

Periodicals

_____

_____

_____

Videos

_____

_____

_____

Reference Sources (CD-ROMs, Encyclopedias, Special Reference Books)

_____

_____

_____

_____

Internet Sources (Use a search engine to locate possible addresses.)

URL — _____

URL — _____

URL — _____

Topic: _____

Getting Organized—Where Can I Get Information? Primary Research Activities and Primary Sources

Who can we talk to that may have information?

Name: _____ phone no. _____

Address: _____

Name: _____ phone no. _____

Address: _____

Where can we visit that may give us firsthand information?

Location: _____ details _____

Location: _____ details _____

What events can I attend or participate in to learn more?

Location: _____ details _____

Location: _____ details _____

What can we do to let others know about our information needs?

School newspaper: _____

Other: _____ Other: _____

What primary documents might provide information about my topic?

What?: _____ Where can I find it? _____

What?: _____ Where can I find it? _____

What?: _____ Where can I find it? _____

Are there any surveys or other data collection I can do that will help provide information on my topic?

What?: _____ Details: _____

What?: _____ Details: _____

What?: _____ Details: _____

Mini-lesson Record Sheet — Library Skills

Students' names

Mini-lesson												
A. Using an index.												
B Determining the scope of a reference source.												
C. Using the table of contents to locate information in a specific book.												
E. Checking the copyright date to ascertain recency.												
F. Learning about the author or the resource person to determine credibility.												
G. Using the library media center catalog: author, subject, title and Boolean searches.												
H. Accessing the Internet or Online services to locate information. Using URL (addresses); search engines, bookmarks.												
I. Using a CD-ROM to locate information.												
J. Accessing area libraries from a remote source (activating a modem access).												

Schedule Calendar

Notes	Monday	Tuesday	Wednesday	Thursday	Friday
Week 1					
Week 2					
Week 3					
Week 4					
Week 5					
Week 6					
Week 7					
Week 8					

Project/Research Planning Guide

Use this weekly planner to organize your work —
to plan how, where, what is needed and the steps to take.

Monday —

_____

_____

_____

Tuesday —

_____

_____

_____

Wednesday —

_____

_____

_____

Thursday —

_____

_____

_____

Friday —

_____

_____

_____

Recording Information
— Taking Notes —

Source of Information

Source #1

Gibbons, Gail. *Recycle! A Handbook for Kids*. Little, Brown, 1992.

Public Library
628.4 Gib

Note Card

Source #1

Trash, garbage, and waste can all be recycled.

Getting Ready for the Interview

Helpful Ideas for Writing Questions

1. Create a word web or list of words about your topic.

2. Use the web or list to write questions to help you learn about your topic.

Consider these points when writing your questions —

- Are your questions clearly stated?

- Do you understand what you are asking?

- Will your questions allow for a variety of answers?

- Will your questions require more than a "yes" or "no" answer?

- Do your questions encourage stories or sharing facts?

- Use telling phrases such as "please tell" or "please describe."

Getting Ready for the Interview

Person to be interviewed: _____

Why is this person being interviewed? _____
_____

Telephone number and address: _____
_____

Time and day scheduled for interview: _____
_____

Questions to ask.

1. _____
_____

2. _____
_____

3. _____
_____

4. _____
_____

5. _____
_____

6. _____
_____

7. _____
_____

Check that your questions ask for an opinion or for information about an experience not available in a book. Don't use experts to do your investigating. Facts usually can be found in a reference and often are more accurate than someone's guess or remembrance. Prepare yourself with facts before the interview.

Evaluate and Assess—1

- Have I located enough information for me to determine the solution to the question or to help me solve the problem?

  yes ____
  no ____

- Or can I modify the question or task to fit the available information?

  yes ____
  no ____

- Have I learned what I wanted to learn about the topic?

  yes ____
  no ____

- Am I ready to share the results of my task or my solution to the question?

  yes ____
  no ____

- Are there any additional questions that need to be answered as a result of the information discovered in this research?

  yes ____
  no ____

- Do I have any problems with this research that I need to discuss with the teacher?

  yes ____
  no ____

How Shall I Tell Others About What I Know

Biography	Itinerary
Book	Letter
Campaign	Magazine
Cartoon Strip	Newspaper Article
Celebration	Painting
Chart	Piece of Art
Community Service	Plant a Garden
Debate	Poem
Decision	Read
Demonstration	Scale Model
Documentary	Scrapbook
Exhibition	Script
Game	Sculpture
Graph	Travelogue
Historical Brochure	Video Show
Internet Website	Yearbook

Choosing What to Do

Criteria to Consider

Project Alternatives	The project that answers my questions.	The most challenging for me to accomplish.	The one that will help others to learn the most.	The one that is the most exciting to me.	Total Points
1.					
2.					
3.					
4.					
5.					

1. Write your project choices in the "project alternative" blanks in the chart above.

2. Rate the criteria statements as they apply to the project alternatives by using a scale of 1 to 5 (1 being low and 5 being high).

3. Total the points for each project.

4. Consider the point totals and other input from your teacher and classmates.

5. State your final project decision.

6. State at least three reasons you made this decision.

_____

_____

_____

_____

Request to Publish on the Internet

To:

From:

Description of project and where requested material will be published:

Permission is requested to publish the following in the manner described above (all items that apply will be checked):

____ include your picture on the Web site;

____ include a quote or quotes on the Web site, from the material you sent in response to this inquiry or from the telephone interview;

____ other, explanation -

Permission granted: ____ yes ____ no

I am 21 years of age or older: ____ yes ____ no (if no complete both portions of the form)

Please print name:_____ Phone No. _____

Address (for records only): _____

Date signed: _____ Signed: _____

****

If person above is a minor, this form must also be signed by the minor's parent or guardian.

Permission granted: ____ yes ____ no

Please print name:_____ Phone No. _____

Parent/Guardian (circle one) of the minor child: _____

Address (for records only): _____

Date signed: _____ Signed: _____

Evaluate and Assess - Final

To evaluate your research task and the product you developed to share your research, ask the following questions to help you assess the effectiveness and efficiency of your task completion.

- Did I locate enough information to determine the solution to the question or to help me solve the problem?

  yes ____
  no ____

- Or was I able to modify the question or task to fit the available information?

  yes ____
  no ____

- Does my product share with others the results of my task or the solution I reached regarding the question?

  yes ____
  no ____

- Did I learn what I wanted to learn about the topic?

  yes ____
  no ____

- If I were to do this project again, would I do anything differently? If yes, what?

  yes ____
  no ____

- Does my project show others what I have learned or decided?

  yes ____
  no ____

- Are there any additional questions that need to be answered as a result of the information discovered in this project?

  yes ____
  no ____

Appendix B

Search Cards

Search Card — Subject

Find a book about:

Giraffe

Search Card — Subject

Find a book about:

Cougar

Search Cards

Search Card — Subject

Find a book about:

Python

Search Card — Subject

Find a book about:

Nurse

Search Cards

Search Card — Subject

Find a book about:

Saturn

Search Card — Subject

Find a book about:

pottery

Search Cards

Search Card — Subject

Find a book about:

football

Search Card — Subject

Find a book about:

George Washington Carver

Search Cards

Search Card — Subject

Find a book about:

mummies

Search Card — Subject

Find a book about:

the post office

Search Cards

Search Card — Subject

Find a book about:

the Civil War

Search Card — Subject

Find a book about:

railroad trains

Search Cards

Search Card — Subject

Find a book about:

inventors

Search Card — Subject

Find a book about:

quilts

Search Cards

Search Card — Subject

Find a book about:

Japan

Search Card — Subject

Find a book about:

turtles

Search Cards

Search Card — Subject

Find a book about:

flowers

Search Card — Subject

Find a book about:

money

Search Cards

Search Card — Subject

Find a book about:

ships

Search Card — Subject

Find a book about:

homeless people

Search Cards

Search Card — Subject

Find a book about:

ambulances

Search Card — Subject

Find a book about:

Kwanzaa

Search Cards

Search Card — Subject

Find a book about:

toads

Search Card — Subject

Find a book about:

tigers

Search Cards

Search Card — Subject

Find a book about:

World War II

Search Card — Subject

Find a book about:

holidays

Search Cards

```
Search Card — Subject

Find a book about:


    football

```

```
Search Card — Subject

Find a book about:


    swimming

```

Search Cards

Search Card — Subject

Find a book about:

food chains

Search Card — Subject

Find a book about:

sharks

Search Cards

Search Card — Subject

Find a book about:

Westward movement

Search Card — Subject

Find a book about:

Africa

Search Cards

Search Card — Subject

Find a book about:

Iowa

Search Card — Subject

Find a book about:

space flight

Search Cards

Search Card — Author

Find a book by:

Laurie Krasny Brown

Search Card — Author

Find a book by:

Mick Inkpen

Search Cards

> ### Search Card — Author
>
> Find a book by:
>
> ## Ann Jonas

> ### Search Card — Author
>
> Find a book by:
>
> ## Martha Alexander

Search Cards

Search Card — Author

Find a book by:

Marc Brown

Search Card — Author

Find a book by:

Judith Caseley

Search Cards

Search Card — Author

Find a book by:

Eric Carle

Search Card — Author

Find a book by:

Kay Chorao

Search Cards

Search Card — Author

Find a book by:

Donald Crews

Search Card — Author

Find a book by:

Donald Hall

Search Cards

Search Card — Author

Find a book by:

Walter Dean Myers

Search Card — Author

Find a book by:

Jeff Moss

Search Cards

Search Card — Author

Find a book by:

James Stevenson

Search Card — Author

Find a book by:

Gary Soto

Search Cards

Search Card — Author

Find a book by:

Cynthia Rylant

Search Card — Author

Find a book by:

Patricia Reilly Giff

Search Cards

Search Card — Author

Find a book by:

Paula Danziger

Search Card — Author

Find a book by:

Ann Grifalconi

Search Cards

Search Card — Author

Find a book by:

Johanna Hurwitz

Search Card — Author

Find a book by:

Joanne Cole

Search Cards

Search Card — Author

Find a book by:

Kevin Henkes

Search Card — Author

Find a book by:

Jean Little

Search Cards

Search Card — Author

Find a book by:

Andrea Davis Pinkney

Search Card — Author

Find a book by:

Virginia Driving Hawk Sneve

Search Cards

Search Card — Author

Find a book by:

Jane Yolen

Search Card — Author

Find a book by:

Laurence Yep

Search Cards

Search Card — Author

Find a book by:

Paul Galdone

Search Card — Author

Find a book by:

Eric Kimmel

Search Cards

Search Card — Author

Find a book by:

Eve Bunting

Search Card — Author

Find a book by:

Gary Paulsen

Search Cards

Search Card — Author

Find a book by:

Gail Gibbons

Search Card — Author

Find a book by:

Caroline Arnold

Search Cards

Search Card — Author

Find a book by:

David Adler

Search Card — Author

Find a book by:

Lois Lowry

Search Cards

Search Card — Title

Find a book titled:

The Gingerbread Boy

Search Card — Title

Find a book titled:

Cinderella

Search Cards

Search Card — Title

Find a book titled:

Blackboard Bear

Search Card — Title

Find a book titled:

Strega Nona

Search Cards

Search Card — Title

Find a book titled:

Why Mosquitos Buzz in People's Ears

Search Card — Title

Find a book titled:

Who's in Rabbit's House?

Search Cards

Search Card — Title

Find a book titled:

Each Peach Pear Plum

Search Card — Title

Find a book titled:

Digging Up Dinosaurs

Search Cards

Search Card — Title

Find a book titled:

Medieval Feast

Search Card — Title

Find a book titled:

Tom in the Middle

Search Cards

Search Card — Title

Find a book titled:

Mooncake

Search Card — Title

Find a book titled:

Bear Shadow

Search Cards

Search Card — Title

Find a book titled:

Shenandoah Noah

Search Card — Title

Find a book titled:

A Garden for Groundhog

150

Search Cards

Search Card — Title

Find a book titled:

Zoo Song

Search Card — Title

Find a book titled:

Leo and Emily's Zoo

Search Cards

Search Card — Title

Find a book titled:

Dinosaurs Divorce

Search Card — Title

Find a book titled:

Arthur's Teacher Trouble

Search Cards

Search Card — Title

Find a book titled:

Ox-Cart Man

Search Card — Title

Find a book titled:

Miss Rumphius

Search Cards

Search Card — Title
Find a book titled: Cranberries

Search Card — Title
Find a book titled: The Hundred Penny Box

Search Cards

Search Card — Title

Find a book titled:

Ed Emberley's ABC

Search Card — Title

Find a book titled:

Amazing Magic Tricks

Search Cards

Search Card — Title

Find a book titled:

Harvey the Foolish Pig

Search Card — Title

Find a book titled:

Up Goes the Skyscraper

Search Cards

Search Card — Title

Find a book titled:

Foxy

Search Card — Title

Find a book titled:

Jack and the Bean Tree

Search Cards

Search Card — Title

Find a book titled:

A Story, A Story

Search Card — Title

Find a book titled:

Arthur's Christmas Cookies

Search Cards

Search Card — Title
Find a book titled: **Little Red Riding Hood**

Search Card — Title
Find a book titled: **Miss Nelson Is Missing**

Search Cards

Search Card — Title

Find a book titled:

When I Was Young in the Mountains

Search Card — Title

Find a book titled:

Where the Sidewalk Ends

Appendix C

Mini-Research #1

A third-grade class went on a field trip to a sheep farm. They watched sheep being sheared and got to feel the wool. The next day one child was found to have head lice. His mother was upset thinking that her son probably got the head lice from the sheep. Is that possible?

Mini-Research #2

In order to enroll in an electronic media class a student must prove his or her age. Since there is an age requirement for this class, the school needs written proof of the student's date of birth. If you were this student, how could you prove your birthdate?

Mini-Research #3

What is the most difficult part of being a
_____ ? What is the best part of
being a _____ ?

Reproducible from:
Research Strategies for Moving Beyond Reporting by Sharron L. McElmeel (Linworth, 1997)

Mini-Research #4

Each year the American Library Association presents the Newbery Award to an author and the Caldecott Award to an illustrator. Who won this year's awards? What were the titles of the books that earned the award for the author or illustrator?

Reproducible from:
Research Strategies for Moving Beyond Reporting by Sharron L. McElmeel (Linworth, 1997)

Mini-Research #5
Construct a three generation family tree.

_____
you

_____   _____
mother   father

_____ _____   _____ _____

maternal grandmother   maternal grandfather   paternal grandmother   paternal grandfather

Reproducible from:
Research Strategies for Moving Beyond Reporting by Sharron L. McElmeel (Linworth, 1997)

Mini-Research #6

Locate the title of a book written by Jacqueline Briggs Martin.

Reproducible from:
Research Strategies for Moving Beyond Reporting by Sharron L. McElmeel (Linworth, 1997)

Mini-Research #7

How many gallons of milk are consumed each day in your school?

Mini-Research #8

What is the average number of children in the families of members of your class?

Mini-Research #9

How many books were checked out of the school library media center today before noon?

Mini-Research #10

In a ten-minute period of individual reading time, how many words are read by members of your class?

Mini-Research #11

In what year was your school established and how many different educators have been principal of your school? Name the principals and dates each were in charge of the school.

Reproducible from:
Research Strategies for Moving Beyond Reporting by Sharron L. McElmeel (Linworth, 1997)

Mini-Research #12

What was the headline in the local newspaper on the day you were born?

Reproducible from:
Research Strategies for Moving Beyond Reporting by Sharron L. McElmeel (Linworth, 1997)

Mini-Research #13

When and how did your family (paternal or maternal) arrive in the United States? Or what is the earliest record of a member of your family in the United States? Tell about the situation surrounding the arrival or about your ancestors' early days in America.

Mini-Research #14

When did you first walk, say your first word, and get your first tooth?

Mini-Research #15

What is the best-selling children's book in your community? Or in an urban community nearby?

Mini-Research #16

How many teachers teach in your school building and what is their total number of years' experience?

<u>Notes</u>

Index